First published in India in 2023 by HarperCollins Children's Books
An imprint of HarperCollins *Publishers*
Building No. 10, Tower A, 4th Floor, DLF Cyber City,
Phase II, Gurugram, 122002, India
www.harpercollins.co.in

2 4 6 8 10 9 7 5 3 1

Text © LHI TV Pvt. Ltd. 2023
Illustrations © HarperCollins *Publishers* India 2023

P-ISBN: 9789356997967
E-ISBN: 9789356997943

LHI TV Pvt. Ltd. asserts the moral right
to be identified as the author of this work.

While every effort has been made to ensure the accuracy of the facts
presented in the book, the publishers are not in any way liable for any
errors that might have crept in.

All rights reserved. No part of this publication may be reproduced,
stored in a retrieval system, or transmitted, in any form or by any means,
electronic, mechanical, photocopying, recording or otherwise, without the
prior permission of the publishers.

Cover design and illustrations: Tanvi Bhat
Cover design: Ramnika Sehrawat

Typeset in Adobe Jenson Pro 11.5/15
by Veena, Bookwatch

Printed and bound in India by Replika Press Pvt. Ltd.

Strange Stories from History

LIVE HISTORY INDIA

Edited by Mini Menon

with illustrations by
TANVI BHAT

HarperCollins*Children's Books*

Get ready to be amused, amazed and delighted by this new collection of quirky stories and see history come alive yet again.

-Ruskin Bond

INTRODUCTION

She is a goddess who tells the story of far-off lands and ancient seafarers. In Gujarat, around the Gulf of Khambhat or Cambay, as it was once known, where you will find ancient ports like Lothal, a four-thousand-year-old Harappan port, Bharuch, which is over two-thousand-years-old, and others like Khambhat and Surat, you will also find temples of Sikotar maa, a goddess who is named after the tiny island of Socotra. This island lies off the coast of Yemen, over 2,000 kilometres away. Even today, the locals, especially boatsmen and traders, seek the blessings of this goddess when they venture out to sea. What is the connection between the island and this part of the Indian coast?

If this goddess captures your interest, you'd want to know how our beloved elephant god, Ganesha, landed up in Japan, or how Cairo came to have a 'haunted' palace whose construction style was inspired by an Indian temple or, further still, how a small town in Punjab has the world within it – from replicas of a French chateau, the grand mosque of Marrakesh in Morocco and the Mughal gardens of Lahore. Read on to find out!

This second book in the Quirky History series, *Strange Stories from History*, seeks to explore how stories connect across geography and time. Like in the first book of the series, we have arranged the fabulous stories under different sections so that you can place them in the right context and savour them more.

For instance, our section on Amazing India has stories that will blow your mind. Did you know that millions of years ago, the Kashmir valley was a giant lake? And what's more, hints of that time, long before humans settled in Kashmir, can be found in myths and legends even today!

In Treasure Trails, we tell you about what can only be described as the most exciting haul of all times. In 1946, a bunch of kids came upon the most spectacular hoard of gold coins when they were playing in a field in Bayana, a village in Rajasthan. The find was so significant that it opened up a whole chapter in India's history!

We also have some interesting Food for Thought for you. Think about this: Why would a king dedicate his recipe book to the king of cockroaches? We delve into a five-hundred-year-old recipe book to find the answer.

That's not it. We also reveal to you a few mysteries that remain unsolved, like that of the army of strange stone men on horseback in the middle of a mountain range in Jammu and Kashmir, and a couple of truly mind-boggling stories, including a mad plan to sell the Taj Mahal!

In this edition of the Quirky History series, we also recognize the contributions of some outstanding Indians who helped us move ahead, quite literally. An absolute favourite here is the story of how we took to the skies – i.e., the story of aviation and how the first rocket to be launched from India blasted off from inside a village church!

Since our stories narrate historical events, several of which are from the times of the British Raj, we have used the old names for Mumbai (Bombay), Kolkata (Calcutta), Chennai (Madras), Thiruvananthapuram (Trivandrum), etc.

India's history is full of the most fascinating, jaw-dropping stories, and we at Live History India are thrilled to be able to bring a slice of this to you through this series. We hope these tales will help you fall in love with history and understand the many different layers that make it.

CONTENTS

AMAZING INDIA

When Kashmir Was a Lake!   17

World's Oldest Zero   24

Gujarat's Connection with Socotra Island   31

A Tantric Temple on a Frog   39

ANIMAL STORIES

The Life and Times of Clara and the Orans   45

The Peacock and Its Magical Tales   54

The Mysterious Horsemen of the Pir Panjal   62

FOOD FOR THOUGHT

Fancy a Tortoise, Anyone?   71

A Lady Who Turned into a Sweet   79

Mango – India's Gift to the World!   83

Why is Butter Yellow?   90

TREASURE TRAILS

Larin: Currency of the Seas   97

An Indian Diamond in the Kremlin?   102

Digging up Gold in a Field   109

FROM INDIA, WITH LOVE

Cairo's 'Haunted' Temple-Palace   119

From India with Love   125

Kangiten: Ganesha in Japan   129

A Maratha Fort in London   134

TRANSPORT

J.R.D. Tata and How India Took to the Skies   143

Hitler's Gift to the Maharaja of Patiala   152

The Real Thugs from Inglistan   157

Vikram Sarabhai and India's Space Odyssey   165

The Task of Measuring India   173

MORE QUIRKINESS

The Plan to Sell the Taj!   183

Paris in Punjab   190

Hazarduari: Palace of Illusions   197

SECTION ONE
AMAZING
INDIA

WHEN KASHMIR WAS A LAKE!

The Dal Lake is the most famous landmark in Srinagar, the summer capital of Jammu and Kashmir. Gliding across its water in colourful wooden boats called shikaras is a must-do for all tourists who visit the city. But did you know that millions of years ago, the entire area we know as Kashmir today was actually a gigantic lake!

It was only around 12,000 years ago that things began to change as the water from the lake began to drain. As this happened, the fertile bed of what was originally the lake became habitable, providing a great place for early humans to settle.

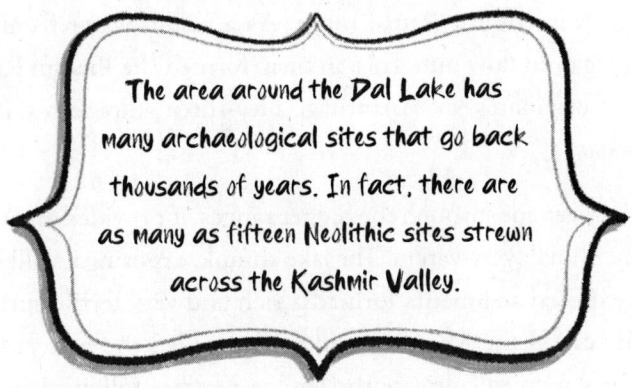

The area around the Dal Lake has many archaeological sites that go back thousands of years. In fact, there are as many as fifteen Neolithic sites strewn across the Kashmir Valley.

The story of how it all happened is amazing!

To understand this story, you have to go back a few million years. We know that the Himalayas are fold mountains that were created when the Indian subcontinent collided with the Eurasian plate fifty million years ago. But it didn't end with that. There has been constant action along the 'fault line' where the two landmasses came together. It is this event that changed the geography of Kashmir.

{ About 2.5 million years ago, Kashmir was a giant, 5,000 square kilometre lake. }

The lake was formed when the Pir Panjal range in the inner Himalayas rose around five million years ago. This led to massive topographical changes in this region. Melting waters from the high mountain ranges were trapped in the Kashmir Valley, creating a massive lake.

Further tectonic movements around 200,000 years ago led to a breach in the Pir Panjal range. As a result, water from the lake began to flow out. This, in turn, formed the Jhelum River, which originates in Anantnag, fifty-three kilometres from Srinagar.

As the river cut through the higher ranges, it provided an outlet to the Himalayan waters. The lake shrank, exposing its old bed. The exposed sediments formed a rich and very fertile surface, locally called the Karewas, and this provided the perfect base for early man to cultivate the land, a practice followed to this day.

Of Myths and Legends

Interestingly, this story is hinted at even in old mythological tales. In India, the points from where rivers start – like Gangotri for the Ganga, Mansarovar for the Brahmaputra and Yamunotri for the Yamuna – are considered sacred. This is true of Verinag too, where you will find the spring and pond from which the Jhelum originates.

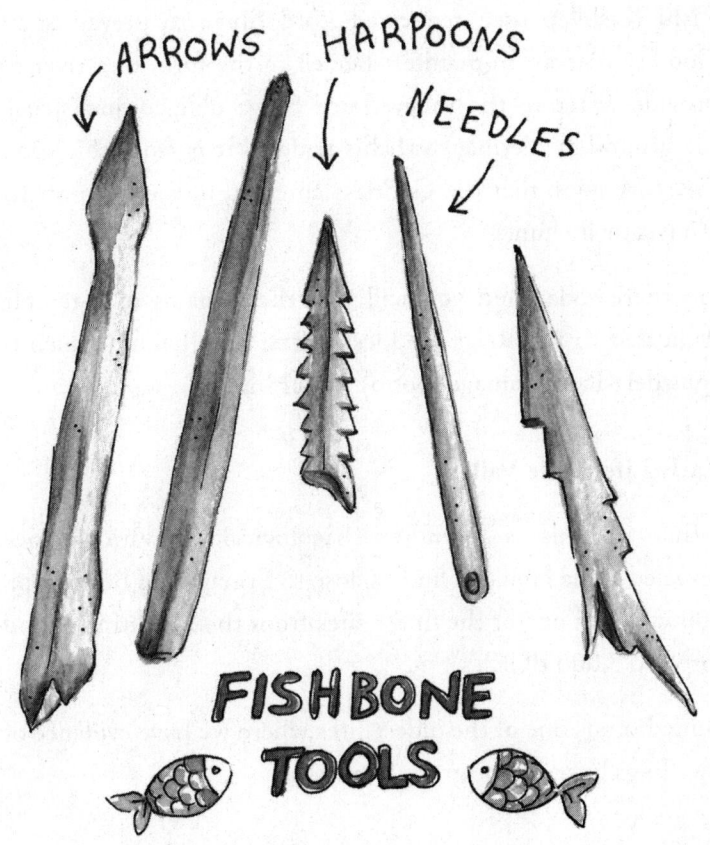

According to legend, Kashmir gets its name from 'Rishi Kashyap', a rishi or sage in Hindu mythology. According to the Nilamata Purana, an ancient text about the history, geography, religion and folklore of Kashmir written in the sixth to eighth century CE, all of Kashmir was a giant lake called Satisar (Lake of Sati). Legend says the lake was inhabited by a ferocious water demon named Jalodbhava, who was a menace to the local people. The lake was drained by Rishi Kashyap while Lord Vishnu killed the demon.

Rishi Kashyap then requested Lord Shiva to prevail upon Goddess Parvati to manifest herself in the form of a river to provide water to the valley. Lord Shiva obliged and struck the ground at Verinag with his trident. It is from this spot, the story goes, that the Goddess emerged in the form of the Vitasta or Jhelum.

Go there today and you will find the remains of a temple dedicated to the River Goddess Vitasta or Jhelum, which is considered a pilgrimage spot by local Hindus.

Early Life in the Valley

While all this is legend, archaeological excavations have revealed some fabulous finds. Close to Srinagar, in Burzahom, you will find one of the finest sites from the Neolithic period (around 3,000 BCE).

Burzahom is one of the oldest sites where we have evidence of dwellings beneath the ground in India.

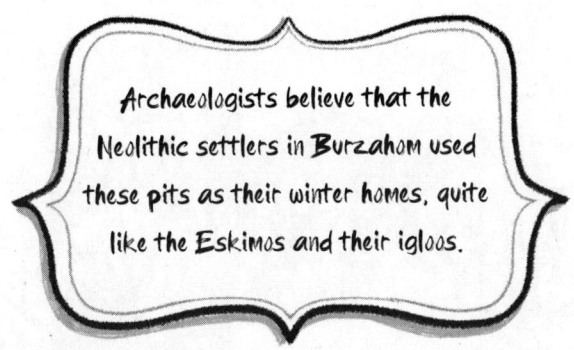

Archaeologists believe that the Neolithic settlers in Burzahom used these pits as their winter homes, quite like the Eskimos and their igloos.

Dug out with stone tools, these dwelling pits have revealed many clues about the life of the communities that lived in Burzahom 5,000 years ago. One interesting find is the use of fine fishbone tools including harpoons and needles. We also know that the dwellers of these homes followed a rich diet, including meat, fish, lentils and barley, which they probably cultivated.

For archaeologists, another stand-out feature of the Burzahom site was that the burials here were unlike any other during this period in the Indian subcontinent.

Humans were buried along with animals, both wild and domestic.

Archaeologists believe that animals may have been killed and buried along with dead humans, and their meat may have been intended as grave goods. These burials were mostly found in the habitation area. Some of the finds at the Burzahom site also indicate how well connected the people here were with other communities. Close ties have been established with contemporary Harappan communities and settlements in Central Asia and China.

Burzahom was continuously occupied for 2,000 years and the evolution in architecture and lifestyles can be clearly seen. Evidence also suggests that around 2000 BCE, the inhabitants of Burzahom were in close contact with China. Perforated stone tools used as harvesters in early China have been found here. In fact, these tools were used only in Kashmir, Sikkim and the Yunnan province of China during that time.

By later periods, communities were erecting megaliths (large stones) like those seen at Stonehenge in England.

Over the years, as many as fourteen other Neolithic sites have been discovered along the Karewa deposits, on the bed of what was once the Kashmir lake. Most of them are near Srinagar, between Anantnag and Baramulla.

It is interesting to note that history, legend and geography come together to tell us of a time when Kashmir was a gigantic lake. Today, the Dal Lake and the rich orchards on the fertile Karewa remind us of a time long gone.

WORLD'S OLDEST ZERO

Shunya, null, cero, kore, sifar – so many words and they all mean nothing. But for those who love numbers, nothing can mean everything if 'nothing' is the number zero. Can you even imagine the world without the zero? Imagine your ten on ten without the zero! How did the world count at all when all they had was one to nine?

This simple circle may not look like much, but the world would be a very different place without it.

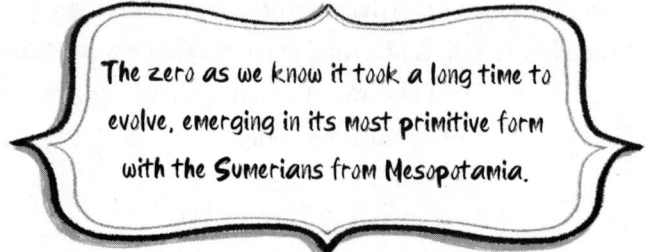

The zero as we know it took a long time to evolve, emerging in its most primitive form with the Sumerians from Mesopotamia.

This ancient civilization, in what is now Southwest Asia, was probably the first to develop a counting system around 5,000 years ago. When they did, they used an empty space to mark the absence of a number in a column or a row.

Later, in the third century BCE, the Babylonians filled in this 'empty space' with a wedge-shaped symbol, to indicate that there was 'nothing' or no number in that column or space. Other cultures, like the Mayans of Central America, used a similar symbol in 350 CE, as a 'zero' marker in their calendars.

We call these symbols 'placeholder zeroes' as they indicate a number's position and value. It differentiates 10 from 100 or 1,000. At this point in time, the zero was not yet a 'number' in its own right, that is, the 'numerical zero' used in mathematical calculations.

These early placeholder zeroes looked nothing like the doughnut-like circle that we know today. Then, in September 2017, mathematicians and historians across the world were astonished when the Bodleian Library of the University of Oxford announced that it had discovered the world's oldest-known written representation of the symbol 'zero'.

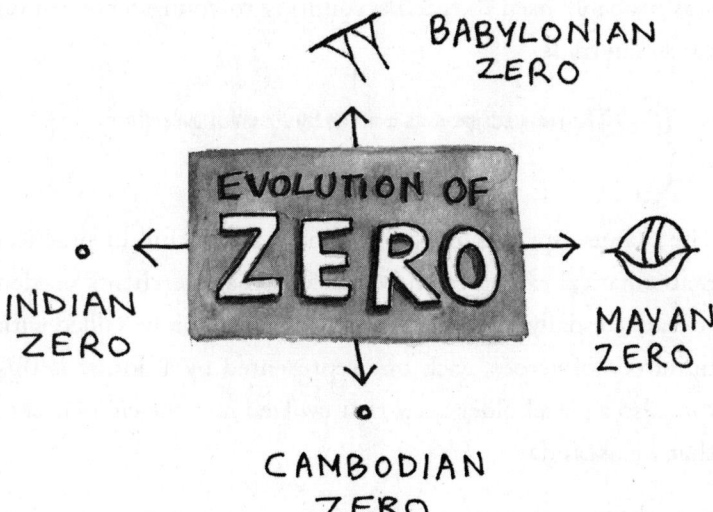

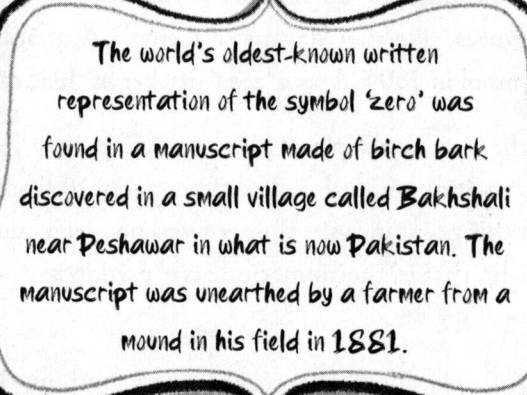

The world's oldest-known written representation of the symbol 'zero' was found in a manuscript made of birch bark discovered in a small village called Bakhshali near Peshawar in what is now Pakistan. The manuscript was unearthed by a farmer from a mound in his field in 1881.

The Bakhshali manuscript was composed of seventy folios or pages, and after it was carefully studied by historians and scholars, it finally made its way to the Bodleian Library in 1902. It was a mathematical textbook-cum-workbook that was probably used to teach accounting to youngsters keen on careers in trade.

{ The manuscript was written by an unknown author in the Sharada script. }

The manuscript was no dull manual. It was full of practical mathematical examples and equations that merchants needed to learn for daily trading activities. As a result, it was filled with hundreds of zeroes, each one represented by a dot. It is this dot, also a placeholder zero, that evolved into the circular zero that we use today.

But what was the world's oldest known zero doing buried in a field near Peshawar?

This mathematical textbook meant for traders was found in Bakhshali probably because the area near Peshawar was a thriving centre of trade and commerce as ancient trade routes to Central Asia passed through the region. Also, the great Buddhist university of Takshashila was situated nearby, which explains why a textbook as sophisticated as this would be found here. Finally, it was starting to make sense.

What didn't add up, though, was why a manuscript discovered in 1881 was making news in September 2017.

{ The reason is there was much debate on how old it was, so experts finally decided to use a method called carbon dating to pinpoint its age. }

When the results were in, they couldn't believe what they had discovered.

It turned out that the manuscript was much older than previously thought. Scholars also found that it was divided into three parts, the oldest one dating to the third or fourth century CE. This made the Bakhshali manuscript the oldest known mathematical text found in the subcontinent. It also contained the oldest-known representation of the zero in the world – and it was older than the earlier contender by around 500 years.

An earlier contender? Yes, and not just one but two!

Before the discovery at Bakhshali, the title of the world's oldest-known zero went back and forth between two Asian countries

India and Cambodia. While the Indian candidate was a temple in Gwalior, the Cambodian contender was a stone stele found in Sambor.

The Gwalior temple, or the Chaturbhuj temple, is a small rock-cut shrine that rests in the shadow of the mighty and majestic Gwalior Fort in Madhya Pradesh. This ninth-century CE temple looks quite ordinary and yet it contains something that attracts mathematicians from all over the world. On the wall of its sanctum is a stone plaque that depicts what was once the world's oldest recorded representation of the zero.

The plaque dates to 876 CE and mentions a land grant of 270 hastas (a unit of land) for a flower garden that would yield 50 garlands for the temple every day. The circular symbol that we know as the zero today appears in the numbers 270 and 50, and it therefore appears not once but twice in the inscription!

But the Chaturbhuj temple lost its title in 1931, when the zero popped up in an inscription on a stone stele in Sambor in Cambodia. What's worse, Sambor had beaten Gwalior by a good 193 years!

Measuring 3 feet × 5 feet, the Sambor stele reads like a bill of sale and has references to slaves, five pairs of oxen and sacks of white rice. The circular zero in the inscription is found in its date, which was 605, according to an ancient calendar that began in the year 78 CE. The inscription was thus dated to 683 CE.

CHATURBHUJ TEMPLE

Here's another twist in the tale. The Sambor stele disappeared in the 1970s, during the Khmer Rouge's rule of terror, and the title went back to the Gwalior Zero. But Cambodia wrested it back in January 2017, when its National Museum announced that it had rediscovered the Sambor inscription.

Just nine months later, the Cambodian inscription had to bow out of the race, as the Bakhshali manuscript snatched the title of the world's oldest-recorded zero!

> The zero as a number in its own right — different from a placeholder — is believed to have been invented by Indian astronomer and mathematician Brahmagupta in the seventh century CE. It was one of the greatest breakthroughs in the history of mathematics. Brahmagupta defined 'zero' as the result of subtracting a number from itself. He prescribed rules on how to use the zero. He also wrote a text called *Brahmasphutasiddhanta*, the first-known document to discuss the zero as a number.

GUJARAT'S CONNECTION WITH SOCOTRA ISLAND

What has a land of flying saucers, dragon blood and eerie caves in the middle of the ocean got to do with the Indian state of Gujarat? Before we reveal this curious connection, let's explore Socotra Island, one of the strangest and most isolated places on earth.

Socotra is a small, crescent-shaped island in the Arabian Sea, at the entrance to the Gulf of Aden. It is a part of the Republic of Yemen, which is roughly 370 kilometres north-west of the island. Socotra is also 100 kilometres east of the Horn of Africa and 2,140 kilometres south-west of Gujarat.

While the island's location has shaped its history, its extreme isolation has resulted in its rare and bizarre plant life. Although the island seems much better suited to aliens than humans, it is home to around 100,000 people. The inhabitants are the descendants of settlers from India and other regions, who visited this exotic place a long time ago.

But who would want to make a weird place like this their home?

Since Socotra is close to the mouth of the Red Sea, it was an important halt for traders using the busy sea route that linked India to East Africa and the Middle East.

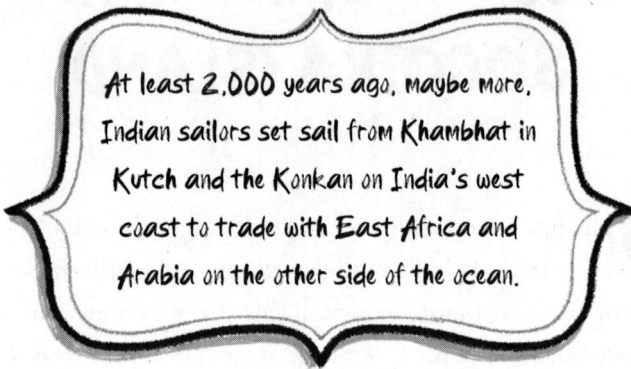

At least 2,000 years ago, maybe more, Indian sailors set sail from Khambhat in Kutch and the Konkan on India's west coast to trade with East Africa and Arabia on the other side of the ocean.

After sailing for weeks, Socotra was the first solid piece of land they encountered before they dropped anchor further afield.

Although relieved to sight land at last, these sailors were afraid to pause at the island to rest. The waters here are treacherous during the monsoon months and ships caught in violent storms rarely made it to safety. It was a fearful place and sailors would have avoided it had it not been such a tempting rest stop.

Even those who didn't halt here were nervous to go anywhere near the island. So they would float small models of their ships to the island as they sailed past it. They wanted to make sure they had appeased the spirits of Socotra! Those brave enough to make a short halt on the island – and survive to tell the tale – started to burn incense sticks in cave shrines there. They said a prayer of thanks for being allowed to make it there in one piece.

When these sailors, mostly traders from Gujarat, made it safely back home, they were so grateful to the 'island goddess' that they built shrines to her in their villages.

> That is why, in coastal Gujarat, you will find shrines to Socotri-mata or Sikotar-maa, a goddess worshipped by seafarers even today.

She is also called Vahanvati Maa, a goddess who watches over their fishing boats and trawlers when they are out at sea. How some things never change!

We know about these early Indian sailors who visited Socotra and those who settled here because they left plenty of evidence

THE STRANGE TREES OF SOCOTRA

in a massive cave on the island's clifftop. Called the Hoq Cave, it has a mouth that is thirty metres high, a belly three kilometres long, and it is filled with spectacular limestone stalactites and stalagmites. Most importantly, the cave contains more than 200 inscriptions in charcoal, chalk and mud, while some seem to have been scratched with sharp objects. These inscriptions are etched into the cave's walls, on rocks and even on the stalactites and stalagmites.

In 2001, speleologists, or experts who study caves, found 215 inscriptions in the Hoq Cave. While some are in the scripts of ancient civilizations such as Aksumite, Nabatean, Early Arabic, Palmyrean and Bactrian, 192 of them are in Brahmi, an early Indian script.

Most of these inscriptions are the names of the sailors who trekked up to the clifftop. Some sailors, probably homesick, wrote the names of their hometowns and villages on the walls of the cave.

{ Some of the sailors' names have religious symbols like a nandipada or a trishul after them. }

In a few places, there are line drawings of two-masted ships with steering oars, just like the ones on the coins of the Satavahanas in India, dating to the late second century CE.

The Brahmi script on Socotra was widely used in Western India between the first and fifth centuries CE, and this tells us how old the etchings on the island really are. Many of the inscriptions refer to the writers as navikas (sailors). Two are from Bharuch in Gujarat, while one is probably from the Port of Hathab near Bhavnagar. The word vani (trader) has also been scribbled on the walls of the cave. There is also a beautifully carved stupa on a stalagmite.

> Bharuch was then one of the most important ports on the west coast of India, so important that it was mentioned in the Periplus of the Erythraean Sea. This was a first-century CE guide to navigation and trade routes in the Indian Ocean and it mentions Indians being inhabitants of Socotra.

Among the 215 inscriptions in the Hoq Cave, one was most intriguing. It was in Kharosthi. Like Brahmi, Kharosthi too was an early Indian script but it was used only in North-West India, in regions that are now in Pakistan. This means that traders from parts of India other than Gujarat visited Socotra.

And guess what? At Ras Howlef on the island, you will find a 'shipping log' inscribed on rocks in modern Gujarati. Going back 350 years, these inscriptions are on stones that look like gravestones erected on coral blocks. They are actually a record of ships arriving at Socotra from the port of Gogha in Gujarat.

It gets even better – some of these were royal ships as the inscriptions mention Emperor Aurangzeb!

> These inscriptions tell us that the journey from Gujarat took fifty days by sea. They say that the ships docked on the island for four to five months and that the number of people on these ships ranged from 100 to 705.

CAVE GRAFFITI

{at Hoq Cave}

The India connection to Socotra goes even deeper. The name of the island itself is believed to have come from the Sanskrit

'Dvipa Sukhadara' or 'Island of Bliss', even though there was nothing blissful about Socotra for those early settlers. Its name may have also come from the Greek 'Dioskoridam', which traces back to Dvipa Sukhadara.

For an island so remote, Socotra has received an unusually large number of visitors across the centuries.

> There are tales that the island was visited by Alexander the Great and that the Ptolemies, an ancient dynasty that ruled Egypt, settled on the island.

These very early accounts also mention the presence of Indians from North-West India on Socotra.

It is also believed that St Thomas the Apostle, who brought Christianity to India in 52 CE, stopped at Socotra on his voyage to the subcontinent. He also converted the island's residents to Christianity, a religion practised there till the late sixteenth century CE.

In the ninth century CE, the Ethiopians occupied Socotra but were chased away by the then Sultan of Oman. In the tenth century CE, the Indian Ocean trade network saw a wave of Islamic traders and seafarers, and many settled on Socotra. But the island's exciting days were not over. Many medieval travellers called it a haven for pirates!

The Portuguese arrived on Socotra in 1507 CE and wanted to set up a base there as it was on the sea route to India.

However, they found life on the island tough. Next, the island passed to the control of the Mahra Sultans in 1511 CE. This was an Islamic dynasty in Southern Yemen, which stayed in power till 1967.

And, of course, there were the British. In these times, everyone wanted a part of the trade in the Indian Ocean trade network, especially India, and the waters around the subcontinent were crawling with Dutch, French, Spanish and British ships. But even the English, who were great mariners, found Socotra unsuitable to live on.

> The British made repeated visits to the island in the early seventeenth century CE but moved on to India. Their next best bet was Surat, where they set up their first trading post and started to build their presence in India. The rest, as they say, is history.

While the world has largely forgotten about Socotra, a part of the island lives on in faraway Gujarat, where Sikotar-maa still watches over fishermen every time they venture out to sea.

A TANTRIC TEMPLE ON A FROG

In the town of Oel in Uttar Pradesh, there was once a king who turned a frog into a prince. Or so it would seem. The king was so pleased that he built a frog temple or manduk mandir, which appears to be riding on the back of a frog!

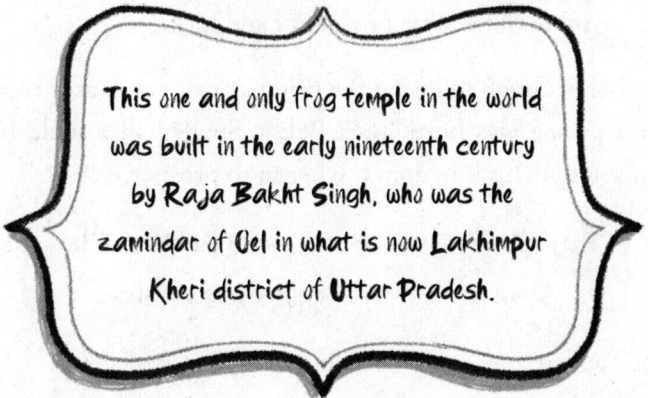

This one and only frog temple in the world was built in the early nineteenth century by Raja Bakht Singh, who was the zamindar of Oel in what is now Lakhimpur Kheri district of Uttar Pradesh.

Raja Bakht Singh was worried about his successor as he did not have a son. Among those who tried to help the raja was a tantric priest. He told the raja to build a temple dedicated to Lord Shiva – but, first, he had to sacrifice a frog and build a frog sculpture. This was a common practice in the tantric tradition, which is an ancient Indian cult. This tradition considers the

frog a symbol of fertility, prosperity and luck.

Raja Bakht Singh followed the priest's advice and, as it turned out, a prince was born. Raja Bakht Singh had a male heir. That's not all, his kingdom too began to prosper.

{ Raja Bakht Singh was so delighted that he built the Shiva temple on the site of the frog sacrifice. }

That's why it appears to be riding on the back of a frog.

The sanctum of the temple is directly behind the sculpture of the frog and can be reached by a flight of stairs. It is square and topped with a dome. It is said that the sanctum is built on a tantric yantra or an octagonal lotus. The outer walls have elaborate carvings that depict tantric gods and goddesses, while the interiors have colourful paintings. There are carved figures of Shiva and Shakti on top.

Tantric rituals are no longer performed at Manduk Mandir but the temple remains very popular among locals. Married couples come here to be blessed with children and others believe that a visit to the temple will bring them great prosperity. They hope that a ceremony performed more than 200 years ago will shower them with blessings even today.

> In agrarian communities across India, there is a strong belief that a wedding ceremony performed between two frogs will please Indra, the Hindu rain god. Thus, such weddings are organized to bring rainfall in times of drought.

SECTION TWO
ANIMAL
STORIES

THE LIFE AND TIMES OF CLARA AND THE ORANS

In July 1827, an unlikely passenger from Borneo arrived at the docks of Calcutta on board a ship that had sailed from Singapore. His guardian, William Montgomerie, a Scottish doctor with the British East India Company, wasted no time in taking him to a colleague, George Swinton, who was associated with the Botanical Gardens in Shibpur near Calcutta.

The mystery passenger spent the next few years of his life at the Swinton residence in Calcutta, answering to the name 'Maharaja'. This is the story of Maharaja (or Sir Oran) and Rannee (Lady Oran), Miss Clara and other animals who became a part of human society.

From the sixteenth to the eighteenth centuries, European powers like the Dutch, the French and the British – who founded colonies all over the world – were enchanted by the unusual and marvellous animals they discovered in these new lands. Since their colonies were on continents far from home, the animals they encountered were nothing like the ones they had ever seen before.

The Europeans were terribly curious about these creatures and took them back home, to study their behaviour and for entertainment.

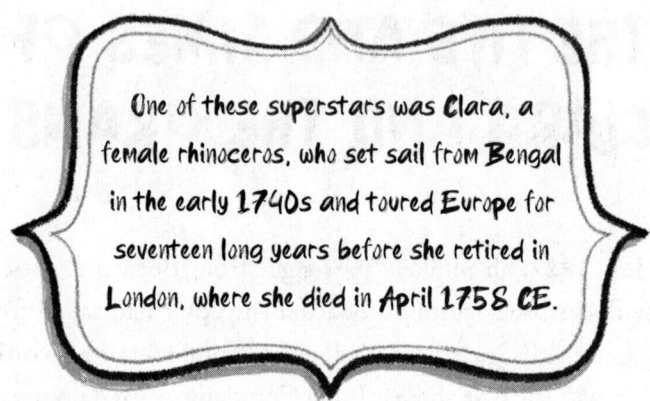

> One of these superstars was Clara, a female rhinoceros, who set sail from Bengal in the early 1740s and toured Europe for seventeen long years before she retired in London, where she died in April 1758 CE.

Clara was only a month old when her mother was killed by hunters and she was adopted by Jan Albert Sichterman, the director of the Dutch East India Company, in 1738 CE. She lived for two years at Sichterman's home in Calcutta before he gifted her to Douwe Mout van der Meer, a sailor and a friend of Sichterman.

Van der Meer took Clara to his hometown, in Rotterdam, in the Netherlands, where 'Miss Clara' became a celebrity overnight.

> Clara was only the fifth rhinoceros to be seen in Europe in over 200 years and most people believed it was a mythical animal, much like the fabled unicorn.

Yet here was one, before their very eyes.

The effect Clara had was spectacular. Huge crowds gathered to see this strange and exotic animal wherever she went, and Van der Meer realized he could make a fortune exhibiting his pet.

CLARA AND VAN DER MEER

So the two of them trotted off to various cities in the Netherlands, before they set off for Germany, Poland, Austria, Switzerland, France, Italy and England.

That's quite an itinerary, considering trains were yet to be invented and air travel took off a hundred years later.

In the eighteenth century, travelling was tough, uncomfortable and even painful, and one had to get around by ship or by road. The rather bulky Miss Clara was carted around in a wooden cage specially built to transport her, and her skin had to be kept moist with fish oil. Given the money he was making by exhibiting Clara, Van der Meer decided it was worth the effort. He wouldn't have got away with it today as there are strict rules on how to treat animals, but those were very different times.

As she travelled up and down the continent, Clara dazzled royalty, nobles and aristocrats in almost every country she visited. In France, she was a special guest of King Louis XV.

{ It was Clara's moment of glory and she was checked into the fanciest animal hotel in all of France – the royal menagerie in Versailles! }

Clara finally retired in London, where she died in 1758 CE, at the age of twenty.

Clara and the Orans were not the only animals publicly exhibited and studied in Europe, although they were among the most high-profile ones. These magnificent animals were named, tamed, studied and even stuffed and put on display in museums and academies that popped up all across Europe. The reason they caused such a sensation – apart from the fact that most Europeans had never before set eyes on animals from Asia and Africa – is that these creatures lived during the Age of Enlightenment.

> During the seventeenth and eighteenth centuries, there was great interest in observing and studying new things in Europe. This was a time when reason and logic were applied to all aspects of life, including nature. People were encouraged to think for themselves, express new ideas and gather scientific knowledge.

Scientists were therefore busy studying new plant and animal species to understand them. And what better than to observe, and be entertained by, animals that were weird and wonderful? It was an opportunity not to be missed! The Orans, Miss Clara and other animals like them presented naturalists, philosophers and even ordinary people in Europe an excellent opportunity to open their minds to something new.

The Orans, a pair of orangutans, were especially important as scientists believed that studying their physique and behaviour could help them better understand what makes us human. Some repeated a Javanese belief that orangutans were, in fact, cleverer than humans – they had the gift of speech, which they deliberately disguised to avoid working!

Sir Oran's journey began in the city of Pontianak in Borneo. He boarded a ship bound for Singapore and then for Calcutta in the care of William Montgomerie, who later wrote that the animal showed an impressive level of intelligence.

> The ship's crew found it impossible at first to keep Sir Oran bound with a length of rope, as he undid every knot they could tie!

'He used to look on attentively during the operation of tying it, and set himself loose with his fingers and teeth immediately,' wrote Montgomerie. Sir Oran was stumped only when the crew used complex knots.

The clever orangutan and his caretaker arrived in Calcutta

in July 1827. Montgomerie handed over Sir Oran to George Swinton, and the animal lived in the grounds outside his home for the rest of his life. He became friends with the bearers who served Swinton, and they, in turn, took a great liking to him.

Sir Oran even picked up many of the mannerisms he saw in his immediate caretakers: he drank out of a tin jug, which he cleaned after use with a towel. After cleaning the jug, he would throw the towel over his shoulder just as the bearers did. A connoisseur of tea, Sir Oran is reported to have demanded four consecutive cups on one occasion!

After the house staff had exhausted their tea quota for the day, they served him cold water, in response to which he apparently 'whined in a peculiar manner, and threw himself passionately on his back on the ground, striking his breast and paunch with his palms'.

Soon after his arrival, Sir Oran was joined by a female orangutan called Rannee, who had been living with a family in Singapore. The two of them were described in letters written by J. Grant, a doctor and senior British official in Calcutta, to the *Edinburgh Journal of Science*.

Rannee

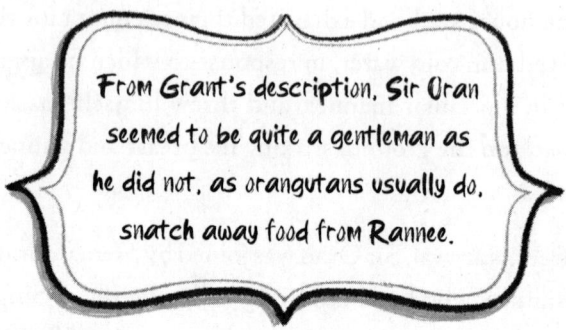

From Grant's description, Sir Oran seemed to be quite a gentleman as he did not, as orangutans usually do, snatch away food from Rannee.

Being sensitive didn't pay off for Sir Oran, as Rannee thought he was a pushover. Grant noted that once, when Sir Oran was ill, 'She appeared at first to sympathize in his sufferings, sitting beside him and bestowing the orang kiss ... but the night being cold, she afterward rather unfeelingly stripped him of his blanket, as an additional covering for herself.'

The orangutans did not live very long in Calcutta. Rannee caught a cold in January 1829 and died shortly thereafter. Her body was sent to Edinburgh, Scotland, and preserved as a scientific specimen. Sir Oran died six months after she did, after repeated attacks of fever.

Scientists who studied his body after his death concluded that 'orangutans do not walk upright as humans do, nor do they walk on all fours'. They figured out something we take for granted today, that the animal is 'quadrumanous', which means it can use all four ('quad' in Latin) feet as hands ('manus').

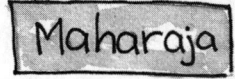

Sir Oran had spent two years of his life entertaining and amusing Europeans in Calcutta, yet scientists claimed the poor chap had gravely disappointed them. He had failed to help them answer an all-important question – whether or not he was a human being, in disguise!

THE PEACOCK AND ITS MAGICAL TALES

Here's a puzzle you can solve in a jiffy: This bird adorns the crown of Lord Krishna. It lent its name to a famous Indian dynasty and it is a favourite image on traditional fabrics. If you need another hint, try this – it's the national bird of India.

The peacock is the male of the species and, unlike the rather plain peahen, it is a magnificent sight. Typically blue and green, it is large in size and as much as 60 per cent of its body length consists of its tail or train. Covered in colourful 'eyes' marked in blue, red and gold, the train unfurls into a spectacular arched fan that touches the ground on either side. Shimmering in sunlight, the fan quivers delicately when the peacock dances, and you can't take your eyes off it till the performance ends.

> If you're lucky enough to have watched it dance, you'll understand why the peacock has inspired poets, artists, writers, royals and common folk since time immemorial. For centuries, this bird has played an important role in Indian tradition. It has been mentioned in ancient texts and depicted in art through the ages.

The peacock is native to the Indian subcontinent and there are ancient references to it being introduced to the West from this country. The Old Testament of the Bible, arguably, states that King Solomon (of Israel), who ruled around 950 BCE, imported peacocks from Muziris, an ancient port in Kerala. Even the Hebrew word for peacock, 'tavas', is believed to be derived from the Tamil word 'togai'.

When the Macedonian emperor Alexander invaded India in 326 BCE, he was fascinated by a flock of wild peacocks in flight on the banks of the Ravi. He was so enchanted by their beauty that he warned his army that if anyone harmed these birds, they would be punished.

> According to some accounts, Alexander took 200 peacocks with him when he left India and they became creatures of wonder in foreign lands. Apparently, people would pay a lot of money just to come and see them.

In India, the peacock has been sacred to many dynasties. The great Mauryan dynasty, founded by Chandragupta Maurya in 322 BCE, is believed to have been named after the peacock ('Maurya' is derived from 'mor', which means 'peacock'). The bird is mentioned in the rock edicts of his grandson Ashoka, the third Mauryan emperor. The seal of the second century CE Kushana emperor Kanishka was a peacock, while the Guptas, who ruled from 320 to 510 CE, issued gold and silver coins depicting this glamorous bird.

Also, the 2,000-year-old neighbourhood of Mylapore in Chennai derives its name from Mayilarparikumoor, meaning 'land of the peacock scream'. Pallava ruler Nandivarman III (c. 850 CE) was known as 'Mylai Kavalan' or the 'Protector of the City of Peacocks'. In medieval times, the Tughlaq rulers (1320–1414 CE) adopted the peacock feather as their state symbol and added it to the headgear of their soldiers.

> Indian mythology is full of legends associated with the peacock.

The most popular one is the story of how the peacock became closely connected with Lord Krishna. The story goes that on Govardhana Hill in Braj, when Lord Krishna played his flute, peacocks danced in joy to the sweet melody. After the dance, they spread their feathers on the ground and the chief peacock humbly offered them to Lord Krishna. The Lord accepted the gift and promised to always adorn himself with it.

Another story explains how the peacock got its beautiful plumage. When Lord Indra was battling Ravana, the demon king of Lanka, a peacock raised its tail to form a protective screen behind which Indra could hide. As a reward, Indra granted the bird its gorgeous blue-green feathers and exotic tail.

The peacock also features in one version of the popular episode of Samudra-Manthan in Hindu mythology, which explains the origins of amrita, or the nectar of immortality. It is said that when poison was churned, a peacock absorbed its toxic effects, thus acting as a protector.

The vahana or vehicle of Lord Kartikeya is a peacock named Paravani. And it is impossible to imagine Lord Krishna without a peacock feather in his headband.

Valmiki wrote in the Ramayana that while in exile for fourteen years, Ram and Sita always watched the peacock's graceful dance together. Many years later, when Sita was abandoned by Ram after his coronation, all the trees, flowers and deer wept, and the peacock ceased to dance. Kalidasa (fifth century CE), in his *Ritu Samhara*, described the bird through the six seasons and its joy when the rains arrived.

The Buddhist Jataka tale of Mahamor tells how the Buddha was a golden peacock in a previous birth. In Buddhist mythology, the peacock is a symbol of compassion and watchfulness. Jain monks once carried fly whisks made of peacock feathers as they were believed to ward off evil.

{ The peacock is also respected by many tribes in India. }

The Mori clan of the Bhil tribe of Central India worships the peacock and will not even step on a peacock's tracks. The bird is sacred to the Jat community in North India. The Warli tribe of Maharashtra fixes peacock feathers in a brass pot to represent their God Hirva and then dances around it. The Koyis of the Godavari in Andhra Pradesh tie peacock feathers to Sitalamata.

> The peacock has been a favourite motif or image in architecture over the centuries, and its depiction goes as far back as the Harappan age (2500-1500 BCE).

Images of the peacock were used to decorate large jars back then. Even the first-century CE Buddhist stupas at Sanchi and Bharhut have carvings of peacocks shown in a welcome pose.

Mughal emperor Shah Jahan (1592–1666), who built the Taj Mahal, commissioned the Peacock Throne, made of gems

The Peacock Throne

and jewels. The envy of the medieval world, the throne had two peacocks facing each other at the top, like the peacock guardians of the Islamic gates of paradise, recreating the Persian belief that two peacocks facing each other symbolizes the duality of nature.

After Nadir Shah's invasion of Delhi in 1739, the Peacock Throne was taken to Iran, where it was possibly lost or dismantled, or used in the construction of the Sun Throne by the Qajar ruler. The Kohinoor diamond from the throne was taken to London by the British and is today part of the Crown Jewels at the Tower of London.

In the nineteenth century, the Mayuri veena was a popular musical instrument in royal courts. Even in traditional textiles, such as the Kanthas of Bengal and Kutchhi work of Gujarat, the peacock motif is very popular. Today, you rarely find a lorry or a truck in northern, western or central India without this beautiful bird painted on its rear!

THE MYSTERIOUS HORSEMEN OF THE PIR PANJAL

For centuries, the rugged mountains in North-West India were a gateway for invaders. They were also a corridor of ancient trade routes. Conquering armies would stream in in search of new territories to rule, and caravans made their way across craggy mountain passes, their precious cargo headed for distant lands.

To guard these mountain passes or *galis* in the Jammu region, an army of horsemen was stationed at different points in the Pir Panjal mountain range.

{ They haven't moved for at least 1,500 years. Some believe they have been there even longer. }

Carved in stone and standing a couple of feet high, these mysterious horsemen are found at the foot of mountain passes or in the main passes themselves. They are usually near a natural spring or a pond. Most of them are off the beaten track and are known only to trekkers and local residents, in places like Gadi Nalla and Nar in Gool tehsil, and the Sildhar area of Reasi district in Jammu.

The most well-known collection of these fascinating stone warriors is near Gool Village in the Ramban area of Jammu. The area is called 'Ghora Gali' or 'Horse Pass', after the horsemen who have been planted here. You can drive right up to them in your modern-day chariot, via the Sangaldan Gool Road.

Head for Gool Gulabgarh, which lies at the point where the Jammu region gives way to the Kashmir region. Here you will be greeted by an eerie sight – scattered across a fairly large area at the bottom of a hilly slope is an open-air museum of sorts. Frozen in time are around 200 mounted stone warriors and carved stone slabs with mysterious symbols. Some statues are standing, others are flat on the ground, while still others appear to be partially buried.

> **Although once thoroughly disciplined, this collection of horsemen is now a rag-tag army. Many horsemen and their steeds were brought here from nearby fields where farmers stumbled upon them while sowing. Some statues are cracked, others broken, and bits and pieces of them have been taken away by villagers to use as benches. Some statues have been used to create boundary walls around fields and homes. Others can be spotted in streams, where villagers use them as washing stones.**

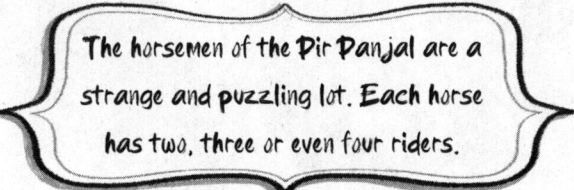

The horsemen of the Pir Panjal are a strange and puzzling lot. Each horse has two, three or even four riders.

Oddly, the carvings are not realistic, as the proportions of the horsemen's bodies are distorted. All the riders carry weapons and are clearly warriors on a military campaign. The sculptures are intricate – the tiniest details have been expertly carved on the harnesses, clothes, arms and ornaments of the riders. There are also stone slabs with reliefs depicting deities and geometric figures.

{ What is most intriguing about these horsemen are their alien features. They are not Indian. }

Historians say they resemble the Hephthalites, a group of invaders from Central Asia who settled in Kashmir and Punjab between the fifth and seventh centuries CE.

Who exactly were the Hephthalites? And why did they leave their army behind?

The Hephthalites came in through North-West India at a time when the mighty Gupta Empire was on the decline. Under their leader Toramana, they took charge and ruled from Kashmir. They left traces of themselves and their culture in the mountain people of the region.

Experts believe that the Pir Panjal horsemen are Hephthalites because the odd shape of their skulls, facial features, clothes and weapons closely resemble those of this Central Asian warrior tribe. Besides, horses were not native to India in ancient times, whereas the Hephthalites were natural horsemen and were used to fighting on horseback.

HORSEMEN OF THE PIR PANJAL

{ There are many theories to explain the presence of these stone warriors in the Pir Panjal. }

There is no doubt that the sculptures mark important points on ancient routes that connected different villages in the region. They were also probably milestone markers or ancient 'signboards' that signalled resting places for weary horses and travellers.

Another theory relates to the stone slabs found alongside the horsemen. These slabs have carvings of what seem to be local gods, leading locals to believe that the horsemen were placed here by the Pandavas from the Mahabharata when they visited the region thousands of years ago.

Today, this stone army has been abandoned. Many of the statues have toppled and are falling to pieces due to exposure to extreme weather. A considerable number were also damaged in landslides during massive flooding in 2014. Although under the protection of the local government, this treasure trove of art is sadly ignored.

These stoic soldiers, who perhaps once led the way or represented the gods, and who have so far managed to conquer time, now face their greatest enemy – neglect.

SECTION THREE
FOOD FOR THOUGHT

FANCY A TORTOISE, ANYONE?

If you've ever wondered what people ate a thousand years ago, or what kings and queens feasted on, here's something to chew on: They ate dosas, biryani and barbecued rats! India's medieval cuisine was a mix of the known and the bizarre. We've dusted off two medieval books that dish out some spicy details about our ancestors' eating habits.

The first manuscript is the *Manasollasa*, or 'Delights of the Mind', written in Sanskrit in the twelfth century CE, in the court of a king who ruled from what is Karnataka today. The king was Bhulokamalla Someshvara III (r. 1127–1138 CE), of the Western Chalukya dynasty, which ruled a large part of peninsular India from their capital at Kalyani (Basavakalyan).

{ The *Manasollasa* is the earliest known non-medical text on Indian food and it was not really a cookbook. }

It was written in poetic verse and is composed of a hundred chapters that deal with subjects like the qualifications of a king, governance and economics, food, music, entertainment and games. It has advice on how to train war elephants, types of taxation and even make-up tips for women! Think of it as an encyclopaedia of life.

And what can be more important in life than food, right? Dig into the third section (Bhartur Upabhogakāraṇa) of the book and you will find no less than twenty chapters on food. There are recipes for familiar preparations like dosaka (dosa), polika (puran poli) and vadika (dahi vada), and some really hair-raising ones like barbecued rats and roasted tortoise. We're not kidding. This is what the elite ate in some parts of India 900 years ago.

But don't get ahead of yourself. According to the *Manasollasa*, it's not only what you ate that mattered but also when you ate it.

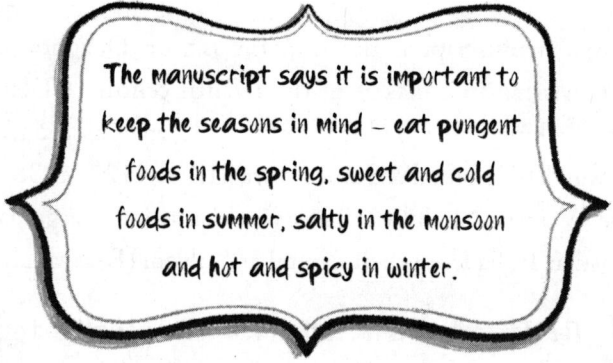

The manuscript says it is important to keep the seasons in mind - eat pungent foods in the spring, sweet and cold foods in summer, salty in the monsoon and hot and spicy in winter.

Another tip: to make each meal positively lip-smacking, combine all the six basic flavours – sweet, sour, salty, bitter, pungent and astringent. Here are some basic combinations: meat with sour items and acidic foods with salt. Interestingly, the most common spice used 900 years ago was asafoetida (hing) dissolved in water. And would you believe it, this spice is still very popular in Karnataka, Maharashtra and Andhra Pradesh.

If you're looking for something light and healthy, salad is a great idea. Our ancestors thought so too. This is what they recommended: raw mango, plantain, bitter gourd and jackfruit in sesame with black mustard-seed dressing. Tempting, isn't it?

And fast food? What did medieval munchies look like? The *Manasollasa* has recipes for purika, small, deep-fried discs popular today as paapdi eaten with chaat. There are also recipes for dumplings made of urad dal to be eaten with pepper soaked in yoghurt, a forerunner of the modern-day dahi vada; and the very familiar mandakas (parathas). Other snacks include peas patties and what seem like five-lentil fritters (modern-day dal vadas).

Our medieval ancestors were big on seafood, or so it seems.

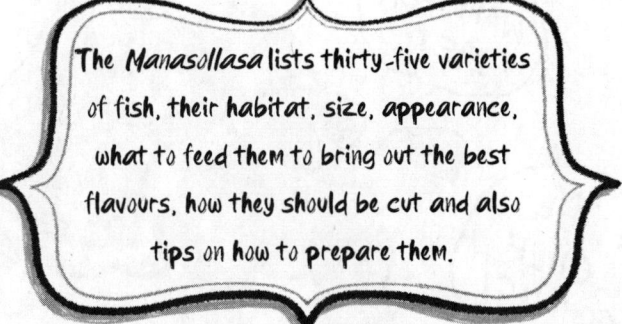

The *Manasollasa* lists thirty-five varieties of fish, their habitat, size, appearance, what to feed them to bring out the best flavours, how they should be cut and also tips on how to prepare them.

There are recipes for fried rohu, popular in North India even today, crab meat (to be cooked in copper vessels only) and roasted tortoise. Yes, roasted tortoise. For meat lovers, the *Manasollasa* discusses a wide variety of skewered meats (today's kebabs). There are also many types of 'black puddings' made from sheep's blood.

Medieval refreshments were not very different from today's thirst-quenchers. Back then, they sipped panaka (a cooling drink for summer), various types of fruit blended with buttermilk (fruit smoothies) and molasses sprinkled with pepper and majjika (spiced buttermilk or chaas).

The text does not focus on just the food. Information about cookware was equally important. Obviously, we don't mean brand names, but what pots and pans are made of. According to the *Manasollasa*, earthenware wins hands-down. If you've eaten dum biryani, you'll know why.

{ *This ancient text goes one step further and recommends serving food in gold or gold-plated utensils. But it admits that this recommendation is fit only for a king!* }

The second book on food is from the sixteenth century CE. It was written by a medieval king and is dedicated to another king – the King of Cockroaches! That's exactly how Sultan Ghiyath Shah of Malwa starts his book of recipes. It's called

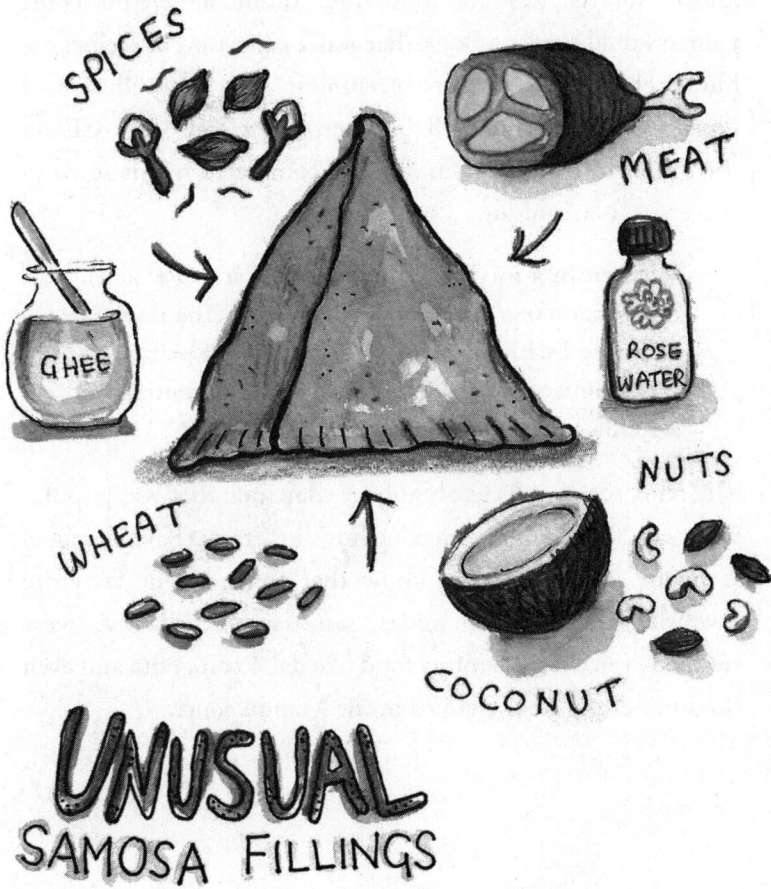

UNUSUAL SAMOSA FILLINGS

the *Nimatnama*, or the 'Book of Delights', and he begins with a plea, 'O King of Cockroaches, please do not eat this, my offering to the culinary world.'

Ghiyath Shah was a great lover of the arts. So, music, dance and painting flourished in his court, giving his capital, Mandu, in present-day Madhya Pradesh, the name 'Shahidabad', or 'City of Royalty'. But Ghiyath Shah was most famously known for his love for food. He commissioned his court painters to illustrate a book that was a collection of recipes for food, aphrodisiacs and fine perfumes. This richly illustrated *Nimatnama* was compiled between 1495 and 1505 CE on the orders of the sultan, and it was completed by his son and successor, Nasiruddin.

> Written in a mixture of Urdu and Farsi (Persian), the *Nimatnama* uses the Naskh script. The book is illustrated with fifty wonderful miniature paintings. Each miniature has Ghiyath Shah in the centre and is followed by a detailed recipe.

The *Nimatnama* tells us about everyday food that was popular 500 years ago. And it is amazing how little tastes have changed! It might surprise you to know that some of our favourite savouries of today, like vadas, samosas and khandvi, were relished even then. Comfort food like dal, kadhi, raita and even the simple lassi were enjoyed in the Mandu court.

> The samosa is believed to be of Central Asian origin and made its way to India via the Silk Route. The result was that the samosas in the Sultan's kitchen contained a variety of what seem to be uncommon fillings: dried whole milk flavoured with spices and rose water, ground wheat cooked in ghee, deer and mountain sheep meat, as well as sweet versions filled with spiced cream and coconut.

But here's the big surprise: not one of the recipes mentions the filling we most associate with the samosa – potato. That's because potatoes arrived in India with the Portuguese a hundred years later. Perhaps they weren't really missed because, in the sixteenth century CE, samosas were stuffed with venison or deer meat. Remember, they were meant to please a king.

> Samosas must have been a royal favourite, for the *Nimatnama* lists as many as eight recipes for this deep-fried snack.

If the sultan ate too many samosas or his love for yakhni (meat stew), spicy shorba (soup) and biryani (richly flavoured, slow-cooked rice) caused indigestion, he would stay away from his favourite foods for a while. He switched to something like millet porridge, which this culinary manuscript lists as a ganvari or gharibi (poor man's) food. How rude!

And here are some surprises.

> While the *Nimatnama* mentions naans, puris and chappatis, popular even today, it doesn't mention the paratha.

While it discusses more than a dozen rice preparations, including khichdi (a rice and lentil preparation), the pulao doesn't feature at all.

The *Nimatnama* is a delightful journey through the mind and the gut of a medieval king. And it ends with an appeal to – you guessed it! – the King of Cockroaches. According to a superstition in sixteenth-century India, cockroaches would leave a manuscript untouched if the name of their king appeared on it. Looks like the plea worked, for the only known copy of this Book of Delights is preserved in the British Library, allowing us to peep into the kitchens of a medieval sultan.

A LADY WHO TURNED INTO A SWEET

You probably know its more famous cousin, the gulab jamun. But Bengal's ledikeni is just as delicious and has a great story.

This mouthwatering sweet was invented in Calcutta in the mid-nineteenth century to please Lady Charlotte Canning, the wife of Lord Charles Canning. But who was she and why did she have a sweet named after her?

Lord Canning was the last governor-general and first viceroy of India. The reason he held both titles is that he served in India when the post of governor-general became that of viceroy after the Revolt of 1857. But it was his wife Charlotte who caught the public's imagination.

{ Lady Canning was a talented painter, an amateur botanist and altogether a very interesting personality. }

Although she performed her official duties as the Viceroy's wife to perfection, she found the routine dull and longed for the great outdoors.

So, braving the Indian climate, she went in search of adventure. Travelling wasn't easy in those days but that didn't discourage

Charlotte. She made many voyages, including a month-long trip up the Ganges, and several treks to the Himalayas. On every journey, she painted the plants and flowers that she saw, and the rich and beautiful Indian countryside.

Charlotte was one of India's prominent artists of her time and created more than 350 watercolours during her tours. Her paintings are displayed in British museums even today.

> But there's something else that Charlotte craved — Bengali sweets!

And there was one sweet in particular she couldn't resist. It is said that on the Cannings' arrival in Bengal in the 1850s, they were welcomed with a grand feast. The dessert at this banquet was prepared by a well-known confectioner in Calcutta, named Bhim Chandra Nag. He made it out of chenna or split milk and balls of dough flavoured with spices, which were then deep fried in a sweet and gooey syrup.

> Did you know that there were many Portuguese settlers in Calcutta in the seventeenth century CE? They influenced the local cuisine, spreading their love for cheese to the local markets. Bengali confectioners adapted the Portuguese technique of making cheese and that's how the Bengali sweet, sandesh, was born! Until then, using split milk was taboo in India.

Lady Canning loved the dessert so much that the sweetmeat was named after her. The locals couldn't pronounce Lady 'Canning' and they ended up calling it 'Lady Kenny'. Over the years, this changed to ledikeni, and that's how it's known even today.

There are other versions of this story. Some say the sweet was first served to Charlotte on her birthday, while others believe it was part of a feast to mark a visit by the Cannings to Baharampur, after the Revolt of 1857.

Over the decades, 'Lady Kenny' has become as famous as the Lady who gave it its name and, since it was linked to a woman of high status, it is still fashionable to serve it at a party.

But the lady who gave one of Bengal's favourite sweets its name died a tragic death. Charlotte was taken ill on her last trip before she and her husband were to return to England. On the eve of their departure, Charlotte came down with malaria and died in her husband's arms on 18 November 1861. She was only forty-four years old.

Charlotte was buried in Barrackpore, in a quiet garden near the river. In the words of her heartbroken husband, it was 'a beautiful spot … looking upon that reach of the grand river which she was so fond of drawing'. Her grave and memorial were later shifted to St John's Church in Calcutta.

If you're ever in Kolkata, you might want to check out Charlotte's memorial, and also try a little 'Lady Kenny'.

MANGO – INDIA'S GIFT TO THE WORLD!

MANGIFERA INDICA

Scientists call it Mangifera indica but the rest of us know it simply as the most delicious fruit we've ever eaten! The mango has been relished so much across the ages that, along with gemstones, spices and the finest muslin, it sailed to other parts of Asia more than 1,300 years ago.

> When the Portuguese settled in Goa, they were so enchanted by the 'king of fruits' that they named a special variety of mango after the first Portuguese Viceroy in India — 'Alfonso' de Albuquerque!

Does that name ring a bell? We thought so, but we'll get to that in a bit.

Since we're discussing names, have you ever wondered where the word 'mango' comes from? Mango is native to India and it probably takes its name from the Malayalam word for the fruit, 'maanga'. The Portuguese pronounced this as 'manga' as they shipped the fruit back home from the ports of Kerala and later Goa.

The mango's sweet and rich flavour and golden-yellow colour have captured the human imagination so successfully that, it seems, even the gods loved the fruit, for it features prominently in religious literature.

> The earliest written reference to the mango is in the oldest of the Upanishads, the Brihadaranyaka Upanishad.

The text goes back 2,300 years and it uses the familiar word 'amra'.

Jains and Buddhists too consider the mango tree and the fruit sacred. It is believed that the Buddha meditated and performed miracles under a mango tree. In one such tale, the Buddha is said to have made a white mango tree appear out of thin air. As a result, Buddhists consider the mango a symbol of knowledge and peace. In the Jain tradition, Goddess Ambika, who represents wealth and prosperity, is shown holding a bunch of mangoes in her hand.

Since the mango tree represents prosperity, kings throughout history have planted it to show off their wealth. Even the

Mauryan emperor Ashoka (r. 268–232 BCE) proudly mentions the planting of mango groves across his empire in the inscription on the pillar he built at Feroz Shah Kotla in Delhi.

But the mango of these times looked very different from the perfectly golden Ratnagiri Hapus that we know today.

MANGO - THE WORLD TRAVELLER!

It is believed that the mango first grew in the foothills of the Himalayas as a wild jungle fruit, and since our ancestors couldn't do without it, they 'tamed' it 2,000 years ago.

They used a process called grafting, which made it possible to plant mango trees in orchards and thus grow them wherever they wanted.

The mango started its travels abroad in ancient times. Buddhist monks from India introduced it to Southeast Asia in the fourth–fifth century BCE. It reached China in the seventh century CE and was grown there abundantly. In West Asia, traders took the fruit to Persia, from where it was shipped to East Africa in the tenth century CE. As the mango travelled, it acquired local names, like the Persian 'anba', which is very similar to the Marathi 'amba'.

The mango was such a celebrity that it never failed to make news among travellers and travel writers who visited India.

> Ibn Battuta, the well-known fourteenth-century CE Moroccan traveller, wrote about how Indians were fond of mango pickles.

Despite its popularity, the mango did not arrive in Europe till the sixteenth century CE. It was taken there by Portuguese traders, who discovered the fruit after they arrived in India, when they sailed into the port of Calicut in Kerala, in 1498 CE.

> It's a long way from Europe to South America, but not for a seasoned traveller like the mango. The fruit reached Brazil in 1700 CE and journeyed from there to Florida, in the present-day United States, in 1796 CE. There's a funny story about how the mango was

introduced to Jamaica in the Caribbean. In 1782 CE, a French ship carrying mango saplings was sailing from the Réunion Islands in the Indian Ocean to the French West Indies in the Caribbean, when a group of pirates captured the vessel and dumped the saplings in Jamaica. What a wonderful bounty for this Caribbean island!

Interestingly, the mango seems to have reached Egypt surprisingly late. In 1826 CE, the king of Egypt, Mohammad Ali Pasha, ordered a consignment of mango trees from India and planted them in his palace at Shubra. The mango made its way to places like Bermuda and the Bahamas as late as the 1970s.

In India, powerful dynasties rose and fell but the mango remained as popular as ever. Perhaps the greatest mango lovers were the Mughals. Memoirs and historical records of Mughal emperors like the *Baburnama*, *Ain-i-Akbari* and *Tuzuk-i-Jahangiri* talk at length about mangoes. Akbar is said to have planted one lakh mango trees near Darbhanga in northern Bihar, in a place that is called 'Lakhia Bagh' ('lakhia' being derived from 'lakh') to this day.

Royal patronage of the fruit extended to horticulture and the grafting of mangoes to produce different varieties, like the famous Totapuri, the first variety to be exported to Persia and other kingdoms. Mughal emperors like Jahangir and Shah Jahan handsomely rewarded their khansamahs or chefs for their unique creations like aam panna, a very popular summer cooler today, and aam ka meetha pulao.

This brings us to the sixteenth century CE and a great turning point in the story of the mango. Thanks to the Portuguese, the fruit would never look or taste the same again – it got even better! As much as the Portuguese loved the mango they had stumbled upon in this great land, traditional varieties in India were the 'sucking' type. These were pulpy, and you had to squeeze the mango and suck out the pulp.

Portuguese traders, who were exporting the fruit from ports on India's west coast, realized that they could make even bigger profits if the mango was refined. They needed a variety that could be 'cut and served' on the table, one that was firm and did not have to be sucked. So Portuguese Jesuit priests began experimenting and grafting on mango plants in Goa between 1550 and 1575 CE.

During this time, they created a large variety of fruits that were given Portuguese names like Peres, Rebello, Fernandina, Phillipina and Antonio. But there was one name reserved for a new variety of mango they had bred – it was called 'Alfonso', after Alfonso de Albuquerque (1453–1515 CE), the man who conquered Goa after seizing it from the Bijapur Sultanate in 1510 CE. He went on to establish a Portuguese maritime empire that stretched from Hormuz in Oman to Java and Sumatra in Indonesia.

While many of the other fruits they grafted are now lost, the Alphonso mango thrived.

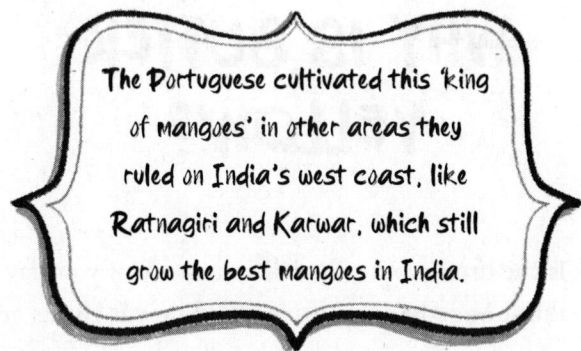

The Portuguese cultivated this 'king of mangoes' in other areas they ruled on India's west coast, like Ratnagiri and Karwar, which still grow the best mangoes in India.

Over time, 'Alfonso' was pronounced locally as 'Hapus', and that's how most Indians know the fruit today.

Experimenting on the mango seems to have been an obsession all along. The famed Dussehri or Dasheri mango is another very popular variety. It is said to have been first grafted in the gardens of the Nawab of Lucknow in the eighteenth century CE, in Dussehri village, near Lucknow city. The story goes that the first fruit of the season was always presented to the nawab.

Today, the mango is cultivated across the world and is a treat, especially in India's blistering summers. It is hard to find anyone who doesn't love its rich taste.

> Poets and bards have written about the fruit, emperors have craved it and it is said that even a pauper feels like a king when he eats it.

It is only apt that Indians should have a deep connection with the mango ... after all, it is ours!

WHY IS BUTTER YELLOW?

This is the utterly butterly delicious story of your favourite breakfast ingredient – butter – and how it got its golden-yellow colour.

Our story goes back a hundred years, to a time when 'Polson' was the only branded butter made in India. It was made by Polson's Dairy, a company owned by a Parsi gentleman named Pestonjee Edulji Dalal.

Before getting into the butter business, Dalal had opened a shop in Bombay, from where he sold roasted and ground coffee, in the year 1888.

{ Dalal's friends called him, 'Polly', which he changed to 'Polson', to sound propah-ly British. }

It was a trick he used to improve his business image. And it worked.

Dalal's coffee shop was doing very well but he wanted to expand. So when he heard that British soldiers were having trouble getting their supply of butter, he spied an opportunity. He opened his first dairy factory in the town of Anand in Kaira district in Gujarat in 1910, and his butter became a huge success. Polson's biggest customers were the British armed forces. During the First World War (1914–18), even American soldiers were eating his butter.

Polson's Butter was so good that, at its peak, Dalal's factory in Anand was churning out five tonnes of butter a day.

What made Polson's Butter such a hit? Remember, this was the early twentieth century and ingredients travelled long distances by train to get to the factories. Since butter is made from cream, and cream spoils easily, Polson partially fermented the cream before it travelled from dairy farmers to his factory. To be absolutely sure it didn't spoil, the cream was also heavily salted. Which also made it oh, so yummy!

But it wasn't only its taste. By the 1930s, Polson's manufacturing plant was using the best technology available to keep up with the demand. By 1945, it had a monopoly on buying milk and cream from dairy farmers in and around the region. Dalal was a shrewd businessman and he promoted his butter as a 'healthy food for growing children'. It's something he probably wouldn't get away with today.

Polson's also buttered up the consumer by offering many interesting incentives.

Each purchase earned points via a gift card. These points were entered into a booklet. The booklet could then be redeemed for various products, from a packet of butter to a refrigerator. It was such a fun way to shop!

But Polson's success was also its downfall. Tribhuvandas Patel, a Gandhian from Gujarat, was shocked at how the company was controlling and manipulating dairy farmers in Gujarat. So he started a people's cooperative movement consisting of dairy farmers and milk producers to take on Polson's. The year was

1946, a year before India's independence, and Tribhuvandas was supported by Sardar Vallabhbhai Patel, who was at the forefront of India's freedom struggle.

> Tribhuvandas persuaded a young dairy engineer called Verghese Kurien to come to Gujarat and run his dairy cooperative. Like Polson's, it too was located in Anand. It was initially called the Kaira District Milk Union Limited and later renamed 'Amul', which stood for 'Anand Milk Union Limited'. Kurien was a meat-eating, alcohol-drinking Keralite but he was determined to make the new venture a success. He became a vegetarian and a teetotaler, so that he would be acceptable to Gujarati dairy farmers and milk producers.

Kurien joined the cooperative started by Tribhuvandas in 1949 and decided to make butter from fresh cream only. He didn't want to use stale, salted cream like Polson did. But his butter flopped. Indians had been spoilt by Polson's fermented, salted butter and, to them, the new Amul butter was pale and tasteless. Kurien was stumped, especially since he thought his product was healthier and superior to Polson's.

The young dairy engineer was forced to do something he didn't want to do – he had to make his butter look and taste like Polson's. So he added a chemical normally produced in fermented cream to his butter, which he then salted. But there was another problem.

> Polson's was using cow's milk, which naturally produces yellower butter, and Kurien was using buffalo milk. To colour his butter yellow, Kurien added a plant extract as well as a chemical additive.

Finally, Kurien's new offering – Amul Butter – was acceptable to Indians. And, in no time, they were lapping it up. It was utterly butterly delicious!

Amul Butter was launched at the time of independence and it freed dairy farmers from a company that had been controlling them, and for very little money. Its success story was much like that of the country's – it offered milk producers economic freedom and it gave the Indian consumer something very Indian. This also played a part in Amul's success.

It wasn't long before Amul exceeded Polson's production and the cooperative ultimately wiped out its competitor.

> Amul became the biggest butter producer in India and it continues to hold the number one spot.

But let's not forget that no matter how much we love Amul and its slogan, 'The Taste of India', the flavour and colour of the butter we relish are the legacy of a company long gone – the salty and yellow Polson's butter.

SECTION FOUR

TREASURE TRAILS

LARIN: CURRENCY OF THE SEAS

They look like something a scrap dealer would be happy to get rid of – old hairpins, bendy fish hooks and small bits of wire. But do you know what a bunch of these small, oddly shaped pieces of silver could buy in the sixteenth century CE? Traders bought spices, muslin, metals, chintz and even precious stones in exchange for them. This peculiar-looking currency was called 'larin' and it was actually a type of coin.

> Larin was the currency of trade in the Arabian Sea and the Indian Ocean between the sixteenth and eighteenth centuries CE.

This was one of the busiest trade routes in the world and it connected Persia, Arabia and East Africa with India and Southeast Asia. Just like the Euro, which is a single currency used almost all over Europe today, larin was a common currency used by traders in the Persian Gulf and Indian Ocean. This region included the entire west coast of India and went all the way down to Sri Lanka and further south west to the Maldives.

LARIN

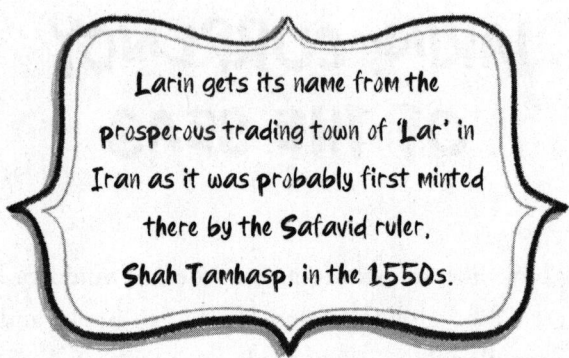

Larin gets its name from the prosperous trading town of 'Lar' in Iran as it was probably first minted there by the Safavid ruler, Shah Tamhasp, in the 1550s.

These 'coins' were made of sturdy silver wire, ten centimetres long. The wire was folded in two, or doubled up, and then bent into a fish-hook shape or twisted like a modern cotter pin. Some were bent to look like hairpins, while others were shaped like a 'J' or an 'S', or just kept straight.

But larins were more than just small but valuable squiggly pieces of silver. Each one was also flattened and stamped with the name of the local king or sultan where it was manufactured. Often the stamp was much larger than the width of the larin, as it was used on round coins, so the impression it made on the larin was incomplete.

Why did larins become the currency of the seas?

First, using a common currency avoided the complicated process of foreign exchange. The calculator had not yet been invented, and instead of converting different currencies every time a merchant bought or sold something, it was convenient to use just one currency.

Second, minting larins was cheap and quick, and the haste with which it was done was obvious. Even then, time was money and it could be put to more profitable use!

Since it was a common currency, the value of the larin was not affected by political disturbances in various countries. Also, its value was linked to the international price of silver, which made it an even more stable currency.

In India, larins were used all along the west coast, from Sindh to Malabar. Yet, oddly, the only Indian rulers to mint them were the Adil Shahis of Bijapur (in present-day Karnataka).

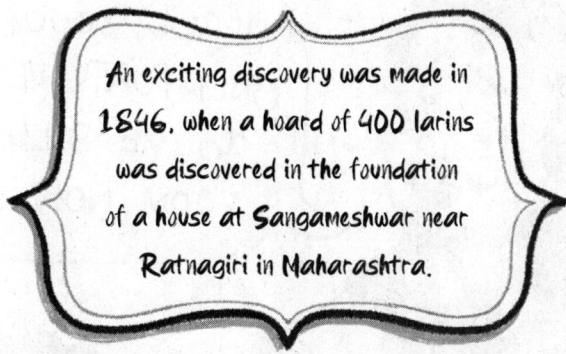

An exciting discovery was made in 1846, when a hoard of 400 larins was discovered in the foundation of a house at Sangameshwar near Ratnagiri in Maharashtra.

Called 'fish-hook money', the hoard made big news among coin experts across India.

These larins had been issued by Ali Adil Shah II and they had 'Sultan Ali Adil Shah' stamped on one face and 'Zarb Lari Dangi (Persian Denomination) Sikka' on the other.

The town of Dabhol near Ratnagiri was an important port in the Adil Shahi kingdom and it was home to the only known larin mint in India.

{ Although larins were mainly exchanged by traders and merchants, they were sometimes also used to pay off important people. }

Around 400 years ago, a French captain called Jourdain who visited Dabhol made an interesting entry in his travel diary. He wrote that the Portuguese paid the 'governor' of Dabhol 2,000 larins a year, to make sure the Portuguese were the only ones who could sell wine there.

It seems this curious currency was used well after the Bijapur Sultanate came to an end in the late seventeenth century. According to official records, larins were used right up to the eighteenth century. After that, they simply disappeared from circulation. According to one theory, this coincided with the 'Spanish dollar' taking over the world of trade. Although it had been in use for a while already, the Spanish dollar had become very popular and was being used in Europe, North and South America and the Far East.

'Fish-hook money' and 'hairpin money' can be seen in museums in India and around the world. In India, head to the Lalbhai Dalpatbhai Museum in Ahmedabad, or the Deccan College Museum in Pune, and marvel at how, for more than two centuries, a snippet of silver had held the fortunes of nations in its twisty grip.

AN INDIAN DIAMOND IN THE KREMLIN?

Behind the high walls of the Kremlin in Moscow is a love story that involves a Russian empress, her devoted lover and a diamond that came all the way from the world-famous mines of Golconda in India. But what dazzled the empress more – the diamond or her lover, Count Grigory Orlov, after whom she named the precious stone?

> The Orlov is a gorgeous diamond set into the imperial sceptre of Empress Catherine the Great, who ruled Russia from 1762 to 1796 CE.

The sceptre is an ornamental staff or wand meant as a symbol of power and authority. Catherine's sceptre was used by Russian monarchs till the revolution in 1917 and is now a part of the Russian crown jewels displayed in the Kremlin Museum in Moscow.

Its showpiece, the Orlov diamond, weighs 189.62 carats. Not only is the stone unusually large, it also has a rare cut and is shaped like 'half a chicken's egg'. It is truly unique.

Catherine adored diamonds and the imperial crown created for her coronation is studded with just under 5,000 of them. But she was no frivolous empress. She was a powerful monarch and her rule is called the Golden Age of Russia.

When not hard at work, the empress had a colourful personal life. One of her lovers was Count Grigory Orlov, who was completely besotted with her. The story goes that when Catherine left him for another man, Count Orlov presented her with a fabulous diamond, hoping to win back her affections. The empress kept the precious stone and named it after the count, but did not take him back! Then she got her jeweller to design a royal sceptre and embed the Orlov diamond in it.

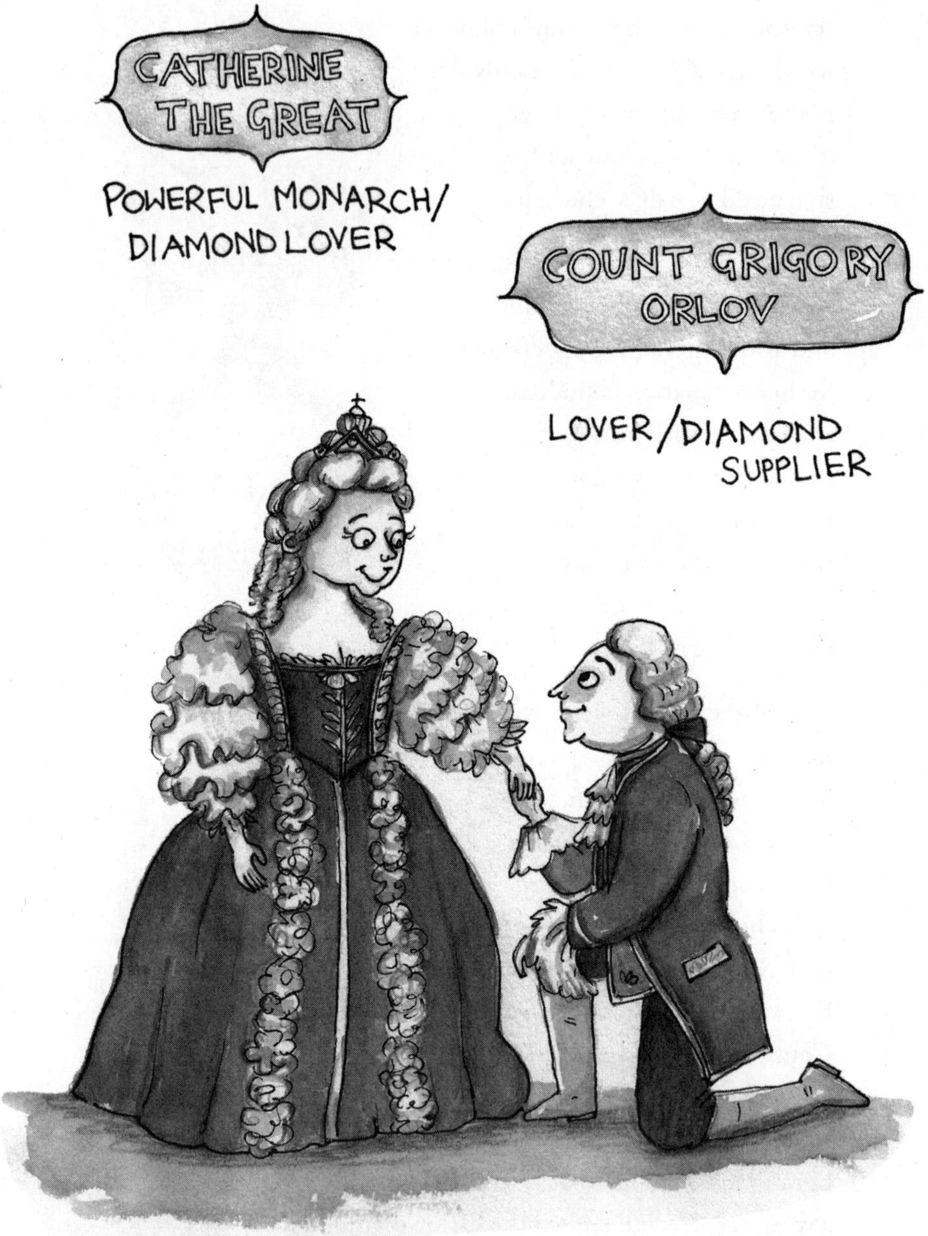
CATHERINE THE GREAT
POWERFUL MONARCH/ DIAMOND LOVER
COUNT GRIGORY ORLOV
LOVER/DIAMOND SUPPLIER

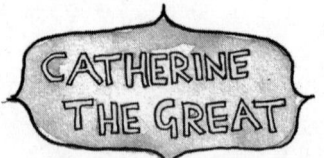

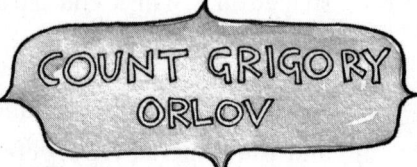

Some say this is no more than a romantic tale. They claim that Catherine bought the diamond herself and made up the story about Count Orlov presenting it to her. She didn't want the Russian people to be furious with her for splurging public money on one of the world's most expensive diamonds.

Since she couldn't resist this diamond but couldn't very well approach the jeweller who owned it herself, she got Orlov to make the deal and have the stone delivered to her. She gave the count a palace in return, although it was not quite what he was aiming for!

Now, the Orlov is not only one of the world's most stunning diamonds, but it also has an air of mystery.

> The diamond was found in the fabled mines of Golconda near Hyderabad in India.

But how did it make its way to Russia? According to one popular story, the Orlov was one of the two diamonds set as the eyes in a giant statue of Brahma in the temple of Sri Ranganathaswamy at Srirangam in Tiruchirapalli district of Tamil Nadu in the seventeenth century CE.

It is said that one stormy night, a French adventurer broke into the temple, stole the diamond and escaped to Madras, where he sold it to an English captain for GBP 2,000. The captain took this stone to Europe and it eventually ended up in Russia. But this is probably no more than an exotic tale spun by a European jeweller to get a good price for the diamond!

What seems like another colourful tale, but isn't, is the story of the Orlov's origin. Many believe this remarkable jewel started life as an altogether different diamond before it became the Orlov. They say it was a part of the much larger 'Great Mogul' (from 'Mughal'), a diamond so breathtaking and so rare that it held the world under its spell. Then, suddenly, it vanished without a trace.

> The 'Great Mogul' was a term coined by Jean Baptiste Tavernier, a seventeenth-century French gem merchant who travelled widely across India.

THE GREAT MOGUL DIAMOND {787 CARATS!}

One of the first Europeans to examine the gems in the Mughal treasury, he wrote about a massive 787-carat diamond he saw there. He called it the Great Mogul.

Tavernier said that this great diamond had been presented to Emperor Shah Jahan by Mir Jumla, a diamond merchant who became the Prime Minister of Golconda, a kingdom ruled by the Qutb Shahi dynasty in present-day Telangana. Mir Jumla switched sides and joined the Mughals, and when he presented himself before Shah Jahan in 1656 CE, he is said to have gifted the emperor many famous diamonds including the Kohinoor and the massive Great Mogul.

Tavernier added that Shah Jahan had this massive rough stone re-cut by a Venetian diamond cutter named Ortensio Borgio, who was in Delhi at the time. Borgio did such a shoddy job that the emperor confiscated all his money and expelled him from his empire! Borgio had reduced the

stone from a whopping 787 carats to just 280 carats. It was sacrilegious!

The diamond remained in the Mughal treasury till the sacking of Delhi by Persian invader Nadir Shah in 1739 CE.

> Nadir Shah took away the Mughal diamonds and other jewels to Persia, and even carted away the Peacock Throne, the seat of the Mughal emperors.

When Nadir Shah was assassinated in 1747 CE, the Great Mogul fell into the hands of an Afghan soldier, who took it to Basra, in present-day Iraq. Here, he sold it to an Armenian diamond merchant named Grigori Safras. In those days, the gem trade across the courts of Asia was controlled by Armenians, who had settled in places like Agra, Isfahan and Istanbul.

And guess who the empress of Russia was at the time. She was none other than the diamond-loving Catherine the Great. Her court jeweller, I.L. Lazarev, also an Armenian, learnt of Safras's diamond but the price was too high. The empress would not agree. Finally, Count Orlov was brought in as a go-between, a deal was struck and, as they say, the rest is history.

DIGGING UP GOLD IN A FIELD

Jitamall, Babu and Tulsi were playing in a field near a small town in present-day Rajasthan. Their maharaja and his men had just finished hunting in the area and after they departed, the three children scampered about to collect the empty bullet casings that had fallen from their rifles. It was an exciting pastime. While looking for these shiny souvenirs in a field, they pulled up a small shrub and discovered a copper pot just underneath. It contained what they thought were buttons.

> What the three children had stumbled upon was a pot of 2,000 gold coins that were 1,500 years old, and their discovery made news around the world.

Experts called it the 'Bayana Hoard', after the town near which it was discovered. The pot of 'buttons' the kids were so excited to find is still the largest known treasure of ancient Indian gold coins ever found in India.

This accidental but incredible discovery was made in a field in Hullanpura village near the town of Bayana in the princely state

THE BAYANA HOARD

A COPPER POT WITH 2,000 GOLD COINS

of Bharatpur in what is now the state of Rajasthan. It was made on 17 February 1946, when there were still princely states in India. Whose coins were these? No one knows, but they do go back to the time of the Gupta Empire, which ruled Northern India from the fourth to the sixth century CE.

Imagine 2,000 gold coins buried in a field, without being disturbed, for 1,500 years!

> The pot had been placed there during the time of **Emperor Skandagupta**, who ruled the mighty Gupta Empire from **455 to 467 CE**.

We know this as none of the coins of his successors has been found in the hoard.

Coming back to our three little friends who made the great discovery – the story goes that the children took the pot home to their parents and, since the adults realized that they were made of gold, they distributed around 300 coins among themselves. Sadly, these coins were melted before the Bharatpur police arrived on the scene. The policemen took away the 1,821 coins that were left, for safekeeping. The poor villagers were forced to pay a penalty of 12,680 rupees for melting the coins without permission.

The maharaja who had been out hunting the day the Bayana Hoard was discovered was Maharaja Brijinder Singh. He realized how valuable this discovery was and so he invited a well-known numismatist, Dr A.S. Altekar, to study these coins. Based on his findings, Dr Altekar wrote the *Catalogue of the Gupta Gold Coins in the Bayana Hoard*, which is the best book on this treasure even today.

In March 1951, Maharaja Brijinder Singh presented this book along with the copper pot and 209 coins to the President of India, Dr Rajendra Prasad, to be displayed in the National Museum in Delhi. Apart from these coins, seventy-eight coins are in the Bharatpur Museum, twenty in the Chhatrapati Shivaji Maharaj Vastu Sangrahalaya in Mumbai, and eighteen at Patna University. The rest of the hoard is with the Government of Rajasthan.

This is not the only hoard of Gupta coins that has been found. There have been seventeen such discoveries in the last 200 years. Most of them have been in West Bengal, Uttar Pradesh and Bihar. In fact, the latest discovery was made as recently as 2013, at a highway construction site in Murshidabad district in West Bengal. But the Bayana Hoard is by far the most magnificent and most important.

And here's why.

> The coins in this hoard have beautiful images and inscriptions stamped on them, and they give us a wonderful insight into the grandeur of the Guptas and their Golden Age.

This dynasty grew out of a small principality in eastern Uttar Pradesh or Bihar around the fourth century CE and went on to build an empire that lasted more than 200 years.

The Guptas ruled from their capital, Pataliputra, which is close to present-day Patna in Bihar. Theirs was a very prosperous kingdom. Under the Gupta kings, literature, science, art, architecture and sculpture flourished. These rulers were excellent administrators and experts at trade. They were also great conquerors and the empire expanded beyond its borders.

The most well-known Gupta kings were Chandragupta I, Samudragupta, Chandragupta II, Kumaragupta I and Skandagupta, and together they ruled from 320 CE to 467 CE.

But by the end of the sixth century CE, the empire was on the decline. It had been invaded by the Hunas, a tribe from Central Asia, and the rulers had begun to lose control over the smaller kingdoms that had formed part of their empire.

Finally, the Guptas faded away but not before they had left behind plenty of evidence of their life and times, including magnificent monuments, temples, sculptures and other artefacts, and, of course, coins. Among their rich legacy is the Bayana Hoard.

{ These coins, with their striking images and inscriptions, reveal so much about this powerful empire. }

Let's take a look at the fabulous stories they tell.

One type of coin found depicts the marriage of Chandragupta I to a princess called Kumaradevi, of the Lichchhavi clan. The reverse side of the coin shows Goddess Durga in a seated posture.

Another coin shows Samudragupta playing a string instrument, with an image of Goddess Lakshmi on the reverse face.

There is also a coin that depicts Kumaragupta I on horseback, holding a sword in his right hand, attacking a rhinoceros. The reverse face has Goddess Ganga standing on a makara (mythical crocodile), holding a lotus in her right hand.

These and many other coins represent some of the most important aspects of the Gupta Empire. The coins tell us,

CHANDRAGUPTA I
WEDS KUMARADEVI

GODDESS DURGA

SAMUDRAGUPTA
PLAYS A STRING
INSTRUMENT

GODDESS LAKSHMI

KUMARAGUPTA I
ATTACKS A
RHINOCEROS

GODDESS GANGA

among many other things, about socio-political events like weddings, the religious beliefs of the rulers of this era and their personal talents.

The coins are struck in gold (called dinars), a mark of just how prosperous the empire was. Many of the kings are shown as warriors, and we know that the Guptas were powerful empire builders. The coins themselves are artistically made, which reflects the importance the kings gave to fine art.

> What is most interesting is that the Bayana Hoard includes the coins of the five greatest Gupta rulers only.

Skandagupta was the last of the great Gupta emperors, and after 467 CE, the empire began to quickly crumble. Repeated invasions and constant battles weakened the kingdom, drained the treasury and reduced trade and commerce. With the kings desperately holding onto what they had left and managing with a treasury that was fast depleting, they paid little attention to art, culture and their coins.

Experts studying the coins of this later period have found them to be of inferior quality and of much less artistic value than those of the Bayana Hoard. There wasn't much variety in these coins, and since the kingdom was no longer prosperous, there weren't quite as many coins struck.

Isn't it interesting that, in earlier times, money was so much more than just pieces of metal that could buy expensive things? Sometimes, it was a work of art.

SECTION FIVE

FROM INDIA, WITH LOVE

CAIRO'S 'HAUNTED' TEMPLE-PALACE

Do you like ghost stories? This one is set in an unusual palace that looks like a Hindu temple built by a Belgian Baron. Called the Le Palais Hindou, or the Hindu Palace, its fantastic architecture makes it appear like something out of a pop-up storybook. It stands in a very posh suburb of Cairo in Egypt. The palace was built in the early 1900s and has been vacant for more than sixty years.

Or has it? They say you can hear lingering music and laughter from parties that lit up the palace a hundred years ago, and sometimes the ghost of the Baron's daughter roams the empty halls. As for the mysterious goings-on in the dungeon, let's not even go there.

> The man who built the palace, Baron Édouard Empain, was a millionaire and he was the contractor for massive railway projects in various parts of the world.

Empain, who arrived in Cairo in 1904, decades after the Suez Canal was opened, was so powerful that when he decided not to depend on banks for loans, he opened his own bank in Belgium!

But he also needed somewhere to stay and nothing less than a palace would do. So he built one. Known more by its local name, Qasr-i-Baron, or Baron's Palace, the palace was constructed between 1907 and 1911, and it soon became the heart of Cairo's social scene. Empain threw the most extravagant parties the Egyptian capital had ever seen, and his guests included the king of Egypt, European royals and American millionaires.

Empain was on top of the world and his exotic Le Palais Hindou was a dream come true. But why did he want it to look like a Hindu temple?

> In the late nineteenth and early twentieth centuries, Europe was rediscovering the ancient world, and there was great interest in civilizations such as those of Greece, Egypt, India and China.

The Baron was not only an expert in Egyptian history and culture, he was also a great admirer of Indian architecture. So when he hired French architect Alexandre Marcel to design his palace in Cairo, he insisted that it resemble a Hindu temple. Marcel modelled his unique creation on Cambodia's famous Angkor Wat and Orissa's temples.

The palace is two storeys high and has reliefs of Hindu gods like Krishna, Hanuman, Vishnu and Garuda all over the exterior. Inside, the walls are painted with scenes from Hindu mythology and the doorknobs are made of gold. Empain built the palace entirely of concrete. Using reinforced cement concrete was a new way of building at the time and the trend was sweeping the globe.

The most interesting feature of Le Palais Hindou is its main tower, which is built like a temple shikhara, where Empain had his living quarters. This section could rotate 360 degrees to ensure that direct sunlight entered all the rooms! Outside the palace were terraced gardens at different levels with unusual plants brought in from all over the world. In the gardens were statues of Ganesha, Nagas and erotic scenes from the *Kama Sutra*.

And what a magnificent sight it was! When it was complete, the palace appeared to rise like a mythical castle from the sand as there was nothing but the Sahara Desert for miles around. Incredibly, this was a part of the Sahara that Empain owned!

Empain had bought a chunk of the desert at a throwaway price from the Egyptian authorities in 1906 and built his fanciful palace in the middle of it. He then developed a township around it that he named Heliopolis. It was intended to be a mark of modern Egypt with wide boulevards, gardens, hotels, clubs and mansions for the city's elite.

Heliopolis was once ten kilometres from the Cairo city centre but over the years it merged with the city as it expanded. It is still very posh and includes a grand hotel, the Heliopolis Palace Hotel, which the Baron built. This now houses the executive office of the president of Egypt.

Le Palais Hindou was home to three generations of the Empain family. It is said that the Baron's sister Helena died under mysterious circumstances after falling from the balcony of the revolving tower. Then his daughter, Miriam, who was suffering from a psychological illness, was found dead in the palace elevator. The Baron himself died in 1929, but despite the string of family tragedies, his children and grandchildren continued to live and entertain in this splendid abode.

{ In 1952, there was a new political order in Egypt and a large number of foreign residents left the country. }

The Empain family moved to Paris and, in 1957, the palace was sold to a group of wealthy Saudi investors. The new owners locked up the palace and vandals stole everything of value, down to the furnishings.

This was when reports of strange goings-on inside the vacant palace started surfacing. At first, these were just stray stories but, in the 1990s, vandals who broke in claimed they had found blood smeared on all the mirrors inside. It wasn't long before the palace was listed as one of the most haunted places in Egypt.

Still, developers started to eye the property and there was talk of turning it into a hotel, a casino or a museum. Even the Indian Embassy showed interest, wanting to convert it into a cultural centre. In 2005, the property was acquired by the Egyptian government, which wanted to restore it. But political turmoil in 2011 delayed these plans. Restoration work restarted only in 2017.

Today, this unique palace in the heart of Cairo awaits a new future.

Did you know this temple-style palace is not the only Indian connection to Egypt? The national dish of Egypt is called koshary, a dish of rice and lentils cooked together. It is nothing but an Indian version of khichdi. During the First World War, in 1914, thousands of soldiers from British India were stationed in Egypt and it was they who introduced khichdi to Egypt, which became known as koshary.

KOSHARY OR KHICHDI

FROM INDIA WITH LOVE

Bungalow. Shampoo. Chit. Typhoon. Which of these is not originally an English word? Forgive us, that was a trick question. All four words are derived from Urdu/Hindi.

Like so many words that crossed over during colonial rule – dacoit, almirah, ghee – these have remained in use in English even today. They're in the dictionaries and you hear them all the time. But, initially, it was a mela. If you'd just arrived in India on a ship and someone offered you a tiffin of kedgeree and chutney, you'd have no idea what you were in for. You might not even realize it was a meal.

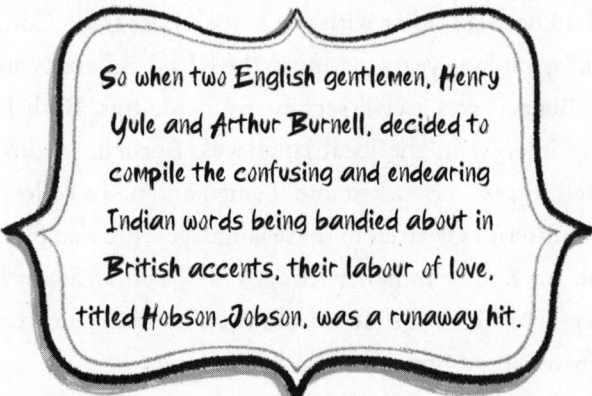

So when two English gentlemen, Henry Yule and Arthur Burnell, decided to compile the confusing and endearing Indian words being bandied about in British accents, their labour of love, titled *Hobson-Jobson*, was a runaway hit.

Yule and Burnell began their partnership with an exchange of letters. In the preface to *Hobson–Jobson*, Yule writes: "We had only met once – at the Indian Library; but he (Burnell) took a kindly interest in work that engaged me, and this led to an exchange of letters, which went on after his return to India. About 1872 – he mentioned that he was contemplating a vocabulary of Anglo-Indian words, and had made some collections with a view. In reply, I stated that I likewise had long been taking notes of such words and I proposed that we should combine our labours."

Yule had been a soldier with the British East India Company. He had spent long years serving in the Khasi Hills of Northeast India. Burnell was a civil servant from Madras. Both had an abiding interest in the local languages. Burnell, for instance, was well versed in Sanskrit and Telugu and had a collection of 350 manuscripts written in these languages. He also published a book on South Indian writing, *Handbook of South Indian Palaeography* (1874), that won him an honorary doctorate at the University of Strasbourg in France.

Yule was passionate about Central Asia and had authored many books. His work, *The Book of Marco Polo* (1871), received the Founder's Gold Medal from the Royal Geographic Society in 1872. That same year, the two men began work on the compilation of words of Asian origin used by the British in India.

> The first edition of *Hobson-Jobson: A Glossary of Colloquial Anglo-Indian Words and Phrases, and of Kindred Terms, Etymological, Historical, Geographical and Discursive* contained 2,000 Indian-origin terms and was published in 1886 by John Murray Publications, London.

Unfortunately, Burnell died in 1882, without ever seeing the finished product or the big success it became among the British serving in India.

Part of that success was because the odd title struck a chord. It was inspired by the Arabic chant 'Ya Hasan! Ya Hosain!', used by Muslims during Muharram processions. *Hobson-Jobson* was a play on how British soldiers referred to the chant as 'Hosseen Gosseen' or 'Hossein Jossen'. The title convinced potential British readers that the book understood how confused they were, and that it could possibly help.

By 1902, the book was already in its second edition. The most recent edition was published in 2013, by Oxford University Press. It has essentially never gone out of style, or out of print.

> In all, there are more than 2,200 words of Indian origin listed in the latest edition.

A handful are explained below.

pyjamas: from the Hindi and Urdu word 'paijaamaa', for leg garment

shampoo: from the Hindi 'chaampo', which means to rub or massage the head

verandah: from the Hindi 'baramdaa'

bungalow: from the Urdu 'bangla', meaning house in the Bengali style

typhoon: from the Urdu 'toofaan', for storm

chit: from the Hindi 'chitti', meaning letter or note

bandana: from the Hindi 'bandhana', meaning to tie

zen: originally from the Pali 'jhana' or Sanskrit 'dhyana', both of which mean meditation

KANGITEN: GANESHA IN JAPAN

The Asakusa neighbourhood in Tokyo is known for its beautiful wooden temples, some of which are a thousand years old. These shrines of the Japanese Buddhist faith are some of the oldest temples in Japan. But there's one temple here that would make any Indian stop dead in their tracks: the Matsuchiyama Shoden temple. This shrine is 1,200 years old, and the reason it stands out is its deity – the idol inside is none other than the Hindu god Ganesha, or his Japanese version 'Kangiten'.

If that's not surprising enough, here's more.

> There are more than 250 temples in Japan dedicated to Ganesha, who goes by various local names such as 'Kangiten', 'Shoten', 'Ganabachi' (Ganapathi) and 'Binayakaten'.

Lord Ganesha is one of the most beloved Hindu deities and is worshipped in countries with a large Hindu population. That's why the elephant-headed god, who is considered the remover of obstacles and the god of new beginnings, has a strong presence in countries such as Nepal, Sri Lanka, Bangladesh, Thailand, Bali and even small island nations such as Fiji and Mauritius.

But why is a Hindu god worshipped in Japanese Buddhist temples? How did he travel all the way to Japan? It appears that Ganesha arrived there in medieval times after making a stopover in China. The worship of Kangiten started in Japan in the eighth–ninth century CE as part of 'Shingon' or 'Mantra' Buddhism. This is a Tantric form of Buddhism, which was founded in Odisha in India and travelled first to China and then to Japan.

> With movie stars such as Bruce Lee and Jackie Chan as brand ambassadors, the art of Kung Fu has wide appeal across the world. But, did you know that the oldest form of Kung Fu, Shaolin Kung Fu, was also introduced to Japan by an Indian monk named Bodhidharma in the fifth century?

It was a Japanese scholar named Kukai (774–835 CE) who established Shingon Buddhism in his home country. A civil servant and a scholar in the imperial court in Japan, Kukai travelled to China in 804 CE to learn Tantric Buddhism that had arrived there from India. He returned home a decade later and introduced several Hindu deities and Tantric Buddhist teachings to Japan. When he arrived in Japan, Ganesha was only a minor deity but he became so important that he features in the *Besson Guides*, religious texts written during this time on the deities of Japan.

Kangiten looks quite different from Ganesha. While the pot-bellied Hindu deity is usually shown seated on a platform and with four arms, Kangiten, a male elephant, is shown embracing a female elephant, which represents his shakti or female energy. This depiction, also called Dual Kangiten, is meant to show the blending of male and female energies. Idols of Kangiten in Japanese temples are usually kept in wooden boxes. Devotees pray to these boxes and the idol is taken out only on special occasions.

The most popular centre of Kangiten worship is the Hozanji temple, on the eastern slope of Mount Ikoma, just outside the Japanese city of Osaka. It is said to have been established by a seventeenth-century Japanese monk named Tankai (1629–1716 CE), who was also known as 'Hozan'.

According to legend, Tankai was searching for siddhis, or supernatural powers, but Kangiten kept putting obstacles in his path, and Tankai kept failing. Then, in 1678 CE, Tankai's master told him about Mount Ikoma, which he described as a 'miraculous place'. To please Kangiten, Tankai promised to make an idol of the 'elephant-headed deva' and declare him the guardian of the mountain. In return, Tankai asked Kangiten to protect him and help him find siddhi.

{ Tankai and his followers built the temple complex in 1680 CE, and it came to be known as Hozanji. }

The merchants of Osaka city began worshipping Kangiten for wealth and prosperity and soon, Hozanji became a very wealthy temple complex. It became so popular that the first Japanese cable car was built here in 1918, to make the temple easily accessible to devotees.

Today, Kangiten or Ganesha is worshipped in around 250

temples in Japan. While devotees offer radish and sake (rice wine) for good fortune, the shops and stalls outside these shrines sell Dual Kangiten statues over the counter, for home worship. It is incredible how similar and yet so different this worship of the beloved elephant god is across countries, across cultures and across time.

Sake and Radish
FOR GOOD FORTUNE

A MARATHA FORT IN LONDON

Did you know that the Maratha island fort of Suvarnadurg (golden fort), which lies between Mumbai and Goa, has a namesake in faraway England? On the fringes of London, in the countryside, is Severndroog Castle, tucked away in a charming wooded area, as far away from the Arabian Sea as possible.

What then is the connection?

Well, there are layers and layers of interesting facets to this story.

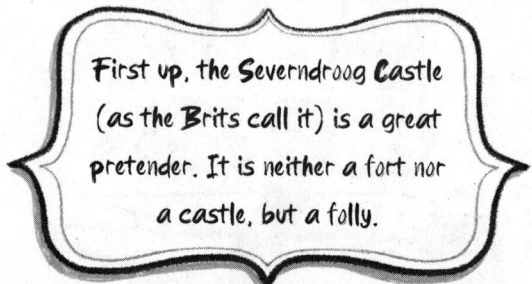

First up, the Severndroog Castle (as the Brits call it) is a great pretender. It is neither a fort nor a castle, but a folly.

Follies are structures that resemble medieval castles, towers and Roman temples but serve no real purpose. Severndroog Castle was built as a memorial to an Englishman named Sir William James, who captured the legendary Suvarnadurg Fort from the Marathas in India in the eighteenth century.

To visit this castle, you have to climb up Shooter's Hill in Greenwich, South London. At the top, there's a quiet clearing in which stands a handsome triangular stone tower with three additional towers rising from each of its three points. All these together form one single tower a little over sixty-feet high.

Mind you, there's nothing Maratha, or even Indian, about Severndroog. For starters, its name is a corruption of 'Suvarnadurg', which the British found impossible to pronounce. And it looks very European. Built in the Gothic style of architecture, the tower has beautiful gilded ceilings, carved figurines, swinging chandeliers and arched windows with white borders and window frames. Why, there's even a fake moat. It seems to be out of a fairytale!

> Severndroog Castle was built by Lady Anne James as a memorial to her husband, Sir William James (1720-1783).

Severndroog Castle

Sir James led a marine fleet of the British East India Company, off the west coast of India at a time when the Maratha navy was at its height. Realizing the importance of protecting India's coasts from foreign invaders, Chhatrapati Shivaji Maharaj, who founded the Maratha kingdom in the seventeenth century, was among the few Indian rulers who gave great importance to their navy. He built several powerful sea forts all along the coast of Maharashtra, which formed a wall of defence. The most prominent among them were Sindhudurg, Vijaydurg and Suvarnadurg.

By the early eighteenth century, the Maratha navy was led by Kanhoji Angre (1667–1729), who was one of the greatest admirals in Indian history.

Suvarnadurg Fort is a massive island fortress in the Arabian Sea. It was important for two reasons. The Maratha navy built their warships here and Angre also used it as a base to establish complete control over the west coast of Maharashtra, from present-day Mumbai in the north to Vengurla in the south. In fact, Angre had an old connection to this fort. His father had been a commander here and Kanhoji had spent much of his childhood in this fort and was involved in daring exploits at sea with his father.

Naturally, the British were always looking for an opportunity to outwit him. They wanted to expand their dominance over trade routes in the Konkan region but were constantly threatened by the mighty Maratha admiral and his men. By

1715, they had made several attempts to capture him. Despite their best attempts, the English could not defeat Angre, who outwitted them at every turn. They dubbed him 'Angria the Pirate', and the Angres would become infamous in the west as 'Pirates'.

> The legend of Angria the Pirate was so famous that it even inspired the character of Sumbhajee Angria in the movie series Pirates of the Caribbean. In the series, he is a pirate who lives in a palace near Bombay.

Kanhoji Angre
MASTER OF THE ARABIAN SEA
NOT ANGRIA THE PIRATE!!

After Angre died in 1729, Suvarnadurg passed to his son Tulaji Angre. Tulaji too was a skilled admiral but he didn't see eye to eye with the Peshwas, the prime ministers of the Maratha Empire, who were now in charge. It was a golden opportunity for the Peshwas as well as the British, and they joined forces to defeat Tulaji.

The joint siege of Suvarnadurg was led by William James and it lasted from 25 March to 12 April 1755. On 12 April 1755, James captured the fort and formally handed it over to the Peshwas. The British took control of it again, in 1818, after the fall of the Maratha Empire.

James enjoyed a very successful career on the high seas. He was only eighteen when he became a junior officer in the British Royal Navy and, at the age of twenty-seven, he joined the British East India Company. Owing to his excellent seafaring and leadership qualities, he was made a commander in the Company's Marine Forces and his job was to protect its trading ships.

{ The capture of Suvarnadurg was James's biggest naval campaign in India. }

Four years later, he returned to England and became a rich and powerful man. He married and had two children, and went on to become a director of the East India Company. He was also elected as a Member of Parliament. James became 'Sir' William James in 1778.

Then, tragedy struck. Sir James suffered a stroke and died during his daughter's wedding in 1783. He was buried in Eltham in south-east London, where he had his estate. To keep his memory alive, Lady James built a memorial in honour of his exploits at Suvarnadurg and called it 'Severndroog Castle'.

Lady James couldn't have chosen a more dramatic spot for her husband's memorial.

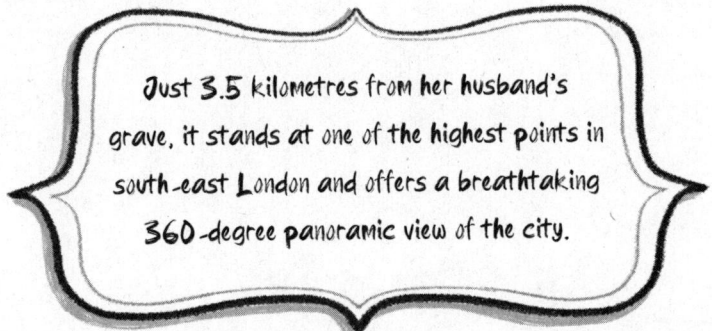

Just 3.5 kilometres from her husband's grave, it stands at one of the highest points in south-east London and offers a breathtaking 360-degree panoramic view of the city.

The memorial itself had to be special. After all, Lady James was a woman of excellent taste and it had to reflect the family's social standing. So she decided on a 'castle', in keeping with the trend to build follies, which dotted the English countryside back then.

But monuments like these are tough to maintain and over the next two centuries, Severndroog Castle changed hands many times. After a string of private owners, it passed to local municipal councils before the Severndroog Castle Building Preservation Trust leased it and restored the monument.

The castle is open to the public and you can climb to the viewing platform for the best views of London and its surroundings.

SECTION SIX

TRANSPORT

J.R.D. TATA AND HOW INDIA TOOK TO THE SKIES

Today, we take flying for granted. While booking flight tickets online and jetting off to destinations all across the globe, it is hard to imagine that 100 years ago, India had no airports! Flying was considered more an act of daredevilry and an adventure sport and, later, a means of travel only for the very rich. And the man who pioneered aviation in India was J.R.D. Tata, the famous industrialist and head of the Tata Group, who went on to found India's national airline, Air India.

But humans have wanted to fly long before that. Gliders, blimps, zeppelins and DIY home projects have, over the centuries, tried to make this happen. Many succeeded while others perished trying.

> But the first true flight took place only in December 1903, when the Wright brothers, Wilbur and Orville, took off in their 'flying machine' at Kitty Hawk in the United States.

A page of history had been turned.

It would be more than seven years before a flight took off in India. On 18 February 1911, a twenty-three-year-old French pilot named Henri Piquet flew a Humber biplane carrying 6,500 cards and letters from a polo ground in Allahabad, Uttar Pradesh, to Naini Junction, a railway station about ten kilometres away.

The plane, made of wood, canvas and steel wiring, took thirteen minutes to cover the distance. There were no crowds to cheer, just a lone postman to whom Piquet handed the bag of mail. Yes, despite the complete lack of fanfare, it was a momentous occasion. India, then under colonial British rule, had entered the world of aviation (and had its first airmail run).

For the next two decades, flights would be used almost exclusively to carry mail around quickly. That might seem like an odd use of such a grand invention, but you must remember that carrying mail was a vital function that millions depended on for official, business and personal use, at a time when there were very few telephones in use.

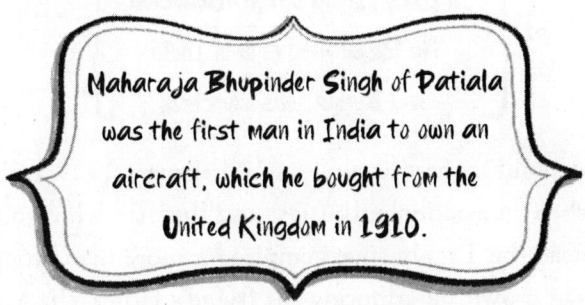

Maharaja Bhupinder Singh of Patiala was the first man in India to own an aircraft, which he bought from the United Kingdom in 1910.

It's odd to think of it now, but until 1924, India had no airports. Flying was so rare that, as late as 1932, when Tata Airlines launched its first commercial flight between Bombay and Trivandrum, its aircraft had only six seats!

In 1924, India got its first airports, in Calcutta, Allahabad and Bombay. In 1927, the government in India, still under the British, established a Department of Civil Aviation. There was finally enough activity in the skies to call for government regulation but it was nothing compared to what we're used to today.

In 1929, for instance, when Imperial Airways (the forerunner of British Airways) introduced international air travel in India, its London–Karachi flight involved four different aircrafts and twenty stops over a period of six to seven days, and it cost GBP 130 (adjusted for inflation, that would be the equivalent of about Rs 7 lakh today). Still, people paid, because by ocean liner, the trip would have taken more than three weeks, one-way.

> In 1927, India's first flying club, The Royal Aero Club of India and Burma, was launched.

It handed out its first licence, on 10 February 1929, to J.R.D. Tata, then an aviation enthusiast and the man who would go on to head the Tata business empire for more than fifty years. Tata had grown up admiring his friend's father, the aviation pioneer Louis Blériot, the first man to fly across the English Channel. At the age of fifteen, he had taken a joy ride on a plane in Hardelot in France, which had inculcated a lifelong love of flying in him.

In December 1929, Prince Aga Khan, the religious head of the Ismaili Muslims, announced a solo air race between London and Karachi, with a prize of GBP 500. The participants were J.R.D. Tata, Aspy Merwan Engineer, an Indian Air Force officer and Manmohan Singh, an Indian who had studied aeronautical engineering and learnt to fly in England. The contest was held in 1930.

Manmohan Singh, whose navigational skills were not very good, twice lost his way over Europe and had to return to

London to start again. So just before the contest, C.G. Grey, Editor of *The Aeroplane*, wrote: 'Mr Manmohan Singh has called his aeroplane "Miss India" and he is likely to!'

Aspy Engineer, only eighteen years old, was to fly from London to Karachi, while the twenty-six-year-old Tata was to fly in the opposite direction, from Karachi to London. Landing at Aboukir near Alexandria in Egypt, Tata ran into Engineer, who was stranded there as he couldn't find spark plugs for his aircraft. Tata gave Engineer his spares and they took off for their respective destinations. Engineer reached Karachi just a few hours before Tata landed in London, thus winning the Aga Khan Prize. Engineer went on to become Chief of the Indian Air Force.

Tata convinced his uncle Dorabji Tata, who then headed the Tata Group, to invest in the up-and-coming field of aviation, and Tata Airlines was born in 1932. The company operated out of a small shed with a thatched roof at Bombay's Juhu airstrip.

> Its first flight took off on **15 October 1932**, piloted by Tata himself, and it carried twenty-five kilograms of mail for the Indian Postal Service from Karachi to Bombay via Ahmedabad.

In its first year, Tata Airlines carried 155 passengers and about ten tonnes of mail. Sometimes, the passengers even shared space with the mailbags! It was still all quite chaotic and informal. At this point, a Bombay–Madras return ticket cost about Rs 256.

If the price seemed exorbitant in those times, the Indian maharajas didn't care. These super-rich rulers were some of the earliest patrons of air cargo and would send and receive some really interesting stuff!

For example, a 1935 article in *The Times*, London, mentions that flights from the Gulf countries carried consignments of the famed Basra Pearls, while the maharajas of Kashmir and Baroda sent mangoes of the best quality to London. Another maharaja even used the air cargo service to send papad to London!

It was early days for Indian aviation and it wasn't just the cost of flying that was holding people back from boarding these new flying machines. It was the fear of actually taking off, leaving the ground and soaring above it, in a machine most people can barely understand even today.

But as the years passed, more and more people took to the skies and, in 1946, Tata Airlines was renamed 'Air India'.

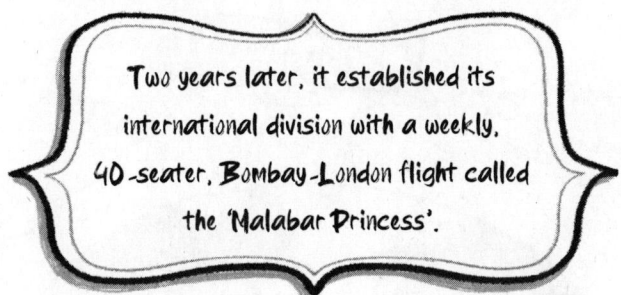

Two years later, it established its international division with a weekly, 40-seater, Bombay-London flight called the 'Malabar Princess'.

For a newly independent, cash-strapped nation, this was seen as a great achievement.

The flying time was cut down dramatically too. The Bombay–London journey took just twenty-four hours, with two refuelling stops at Cairo and Geneva. Advertisements in the newspapers recorded the ticket price as Rs 1,720. Passengers included celebrities such as cricketer Duleepsinhji, travelling to watch the Ashes in London; his cousin Maharaja Digvijaysinhji of Nawanagar; Indian cyclists H.B. Malcolm and R.R. Noble, who were representing India at the Olympics in London; and J.R.D. Tata himself.

{ In 1953, the Indian government took over Air India, and, to honour Tata's contribution, retained him as the company's chairman. }

Under Tata, Air India was considered one of the world's best airlines in terms of luxury, comfort, service and punctuality.

In 1960, with a fleet of six Boeing 707s, Air India became the world's first airline to fly fully into the 'jet age'. Tata continued to head Air India until 1977, when he was removed for political reasons after the government changed. Soon, this airline, which had notched up so many firsts, began to slip and slide, and then plummet.

> In 1990, Air India made it to the Guinness Book of World Records for the largest evacuation effort by a civil airline, when it flew more than 1,11,000 people from Amman in Jordan to Bombay in fifty-nine days, operating 488 flights just before the first Gulf War.

After many ups and downs in its fortunes, Air India went back to the Tata Group, who took charge and ownership of the airline in January 2022.

Today, hundreds of thousands of Indians board flights that crisscross the nation and the world, and it's strange to even think of a time when the skies were, well, empty.

HITLER'S GIFT TO THE MAHARAJA OF PATIALA

For all their power and prestige, India's charming princes and nawabs were just boys who loved expensive toys. But Maharaja Bhupinder Singh of Patiala owned something none of the other princes could have – a rare Maybach car gifted to him by the infamous Nazi German dictator Adolf Hitler.

The ultra-luxury, German-made Maybach was one of only six of its kind in the world, and Bhupinder Singh (r. 1900–38) had one in his garage at the Moti Bagh Palace in Patiala, Punjab. The cream-coloured Maybach was long and sleek with elegant curves, and was dressed in maroon upholstery. It was a drophead, that is, it had a folding roof that rolled all the way back.

Bhupinder Singh was the eighth Maharaja of Patiala, a princely state in Punjab founded in 1763 CE, after the decline of Mughal power. It rose to prominence due to its support to the British during the Revolt of 1857. The vast income from the fertile plains of Punjab turned it into one of the wealthiest and most powerful kingdoms in India, and the Patiala rulers supported the British during their wars in Afghanistan, China and the Middle East.

> Maharaja Bhupinder Singh had a big reputation to match. He had been declared the maharaja at the tender age of nine in 1900. On assuming power at the age of eighteen, Bhupinder Singh went on to become one of the most influential princes in India.

The maharaja was pleased as punch to have the sleek Maybach! He loved the good life, especially jewels, sports cars and vintage cars. The vehicles he collected were parked in a garage that looked more like a giant warehouse, and the most precious cars in it were twenty-seven Rolls Royces. Now they had a Maybach for company!

> Maharaja Bhupinder Singh's father, Maharaja Rajinder Singh, was among the first few to own a car in India. Purchased in 1892 CE, it was the French-made De Dion Bouton steam car and it had the registration number plate 'O'.

Maharaja Bhupinder Singh was also a first-class cricketer and captained the Indian team that visited England in 1911. Why, he even donated the trophy for the prestigious Ranji Trophy, a tournament named after his cricketer-friend, Maharaja Ranjitsinhji of Nawanagar.

Politics was another playground for the colourful Maharaja, who was very influential in both India and Europe. He was a personal friend of the kings of England, Spain, Sweden, Norway and many other nations, and this is probably why Adolf Hitler gifted him a Maybach in 1935, when the maharaja was visiting Germany. The only other rulers who were gifted cars by Hitler were King Farouk of Egypt and the Rana of Nepal.

We will probably never know what Hitler and Bhupinder Singh discussed when they met but it is believed that the German dictator hoped that Maharaja Bhupinder Singh would remain neutral and not support his friends, the British, in the event of a war between Germany and the British Empire. He was probably hoping to secure India's support against British imperialism.

So the Maybach was probably a gesture of diplomacy, not friendship, but Bhupinder Singh was thrilled to have it anyway.

The story of this gift is recounted by Maharaja Bhupinder Singh's grandson, Raja Malvinder Singh, in the book *The Automobiles of the Maharajas* by historian Sharada Dwivedi, published in 2003. In the book, he says: 'My grandfather Maharaja Bhupinder Singh went to Germany in 1935 and asked to see Adolf Hitler who very reluctantly gave him 10 to 15 minutes. They got into conversation, one thing led to another and 15 minutes became 30 and then 60. The Führer asked grandfather to stay on for lunch and then asked him to come back the next day and then a third day. On the third day, he gave him German weapons like Lignose, Walther and Luger pistols and a magnificent Maybach.'

The Maybach was a ceremonial vehicle – a very large car with an enormous bonnet. It could seat two in front and three at the back. It also had foot rests for passengers. This extraordinary car was shipped to India and kept in the garage at the Moti Bagh Palace in Patiala.

{ When the Second World War broke out, the Maybach was hidden within the palace and never used. }

The Nazis under Hitler were spreading terror across Europe, and Maharaja Bhupinder Singh did not want people to think that he and the dictator were friends.

After Bhupinder Singh died, he was succeeded by his son, Maharaja Yadavindra Singh. In 1947, India became independent and the princely states merged with the Indian Union. Like other princely families, the Patiala royal family too sold its vast possessions. Many priceless items were simply given away, including Hitler's gift – the Maybach.

In the book, Raja Malvinder Singh recalls how the Patiala family lost its Maybach in 1967:

'I think it was the only Maybach of its kind that survived the war. I was sitting one day in Patiala House, Delhi, reading a comic when my father walked in with Sardar Sukhjit Singh Majithia after a game of Golf. The ADC (Aide De Camp)

came and said that Sardar Satyajit Singh had come to see my father. I was minding my own business but listening to what they were saying.

'After a while, Sardar Satyajit Singh, an ADC to my father, said, "Sir, I have come to ask a favour of you. You have this Maybach which you have never used. Can I buy it from you?" My father said, "I am not selling any cars, but if you want it as a gift, you can take it."

'We had an Australian named Harvey who was in charge of the garages and Sardar Satyajit said, "Sir, could you give it to me in writing as Harvey won't give it to me." So my father dictated a letter to the stenographer, signed it and the next day Satyajit drove to Patiala and picked up the Maybach. He eventually sold it and it is now with a private collector in America and probably worth close to 5 million dollars.'

In 2015, the Maybach suddenly resurfaced at an auction in Denmark. In a rather unimpressive end to such a remarkable tale, it was sold to an unnamed buyer for an undisclosed sum – and no one even knows where it is. It is an important souvenir of princely India, lost perhaps forever.

THE REAL THUGS FROM INGLISTAN

You know that classic image of a pirate – fearsome eye patch, three-cornered hat or bandana, spitting tobacco as he exclaims 'shiver me timbers'? Yeah, that never really happened. Real pirates were savage outlaws who had no time for niceties. They were too busy plundering trading vessels on the high seas, murdering their crew and snatching their treasure. And the Arabian Sea was no different.

> These seafaring outlaws discovered the bounty to be had in these waters as European trading ships sailed into the Arabian Sea after the Portuguese explorer Vasco da Gama discovered the sea route to India in 1498. Sea trade flourished between India's west coast and East Africa and the Middle East.

Piracy here peaked between 1650 CE and 1720 CE – this is called the Golden Age of Piracy – and it was the English from 'Inglistan', or England, who were the most feared pirates around in these waters. They regularly plundered the ships of the Mughals, whose empire was one of the richest in the world.

In the seventeenth century, Surat was the richest and most important port in India. It was here that the British East India Company first arrived when they came to India, and by 1619 CE, they had set up a trading post there. Surat was also the main port that linked the Mughal Empire with the Middle East and West Asia, and the sea route between these two regions was one of the busiest trade highways in the world. It was also from Surat that Muslims from all over India set sail for the annual Hajj pilgrimage in Mecca.

> The ships carrying Hajj pilgrims were called the 'Mecca fleet' and were regularly raided by pirates in the Arabian Sea.

When they set off with pilgrims, they were also laden with exports such as cotton, silk, wheat and carpets. On their return, their holds would be filled with massive amounts of gold and silver bars, ingots and coins, earned in exchange for their precious cargo.

Naturally, these goings-on attracted the attention of pirates, especially a man named Henry Avery. He wasn't a pirate for long but Avery pulled off one of the most dramatic and brutal acts of piracy on the high seas. It earned him the nickname 'King of Pirates' and some even say he was the richest pirate in history.

Henry Avery
KING OF PIRATES!

Avery started his career as a sailor in the British Royal Navy. He went on to work for an English company involved in the African slave trade, and finally joined a British company that teamed up with the Spanish to attack French vessels in the West Indies.

While he was serving on one of these vessels in 1694 CE, a mutiny broke out on the ship. Avery seized the vessel, renamed it *Fancy*, and even modified it to make it one of the fastest ships sailing the Atlantic. Avery made off with the ship and struck out on his own. And he couldn't have picked a more dramatic target for his first major mission – the *Ganj-i-Sawai*, the star of the Mecca fleet, and the largest Mughal ship in the port of Surat. Imagine the size of her cargo and the treasure in her holds!

In August 1695 CE, the *Ganj-i-Sawai* was returning from Mecca and was carrying so much gold and silver that it was being escorted by no less than twenty-four ships. It was also bringing back pilgrims. Avery and his men lay in wait on board the *Fancy* and a few smaller vessels at the mouth of the Red Sea. As the *Ganj-i-Sawai* approached, the pirates targeted one of her escort vessels and caught up with the ship only the following afternoon. The *Ganj-i-Sawai* was far superior to the *Fancy*. She also had more guns and more men but the crew was no match for the savage pirates.

The crew of the two ships engaged in a ferocious battle and, for the next few hours, the air was filled with smoke and the deafening roar of canons. Then one of the cannons on the *Ganj-i-Sawai* accidentally exploded, killing several men and setting a part of the ship on fire. With the crew distracted, Avery and his pirates climbed on board and started to wrestle with the Indian sailors. When it was clear that the pirates were winning, the captain of the *Ganj-i-Sawai* hid below the decks with the women!

It is said that Avery and his crew were able to find the treasure only after torturing the passengers and the crew for three days.

{ Today, the booty on board the *Ganj-i-Sawai* would have amounted to a mind-boggling Rs 1,100 crore! And this was more than 300 years ago. }

This saga on the high seas was far from over. While the pirates were plundering the *Ganj-i-Sawai*, nine crew members escaped on a small boat and reached Surat. The governor of Surat sent out a search party for the *Ganj-i-Sawai*, with boats borrowed from the French and the Dutch, but they could not locate the ship. Then, on 12 September 1695 CE, the *Ganj-i-Sawai* finally pulled into the port of Surat.

After the battered survivors were hauled ashore and narrated their horrifying story, a bloodthirsty mob surrounded the English trading post in Surat. They were determined to take revenge. No one knew for sure but they suspected that Avery was hand in glove with the East India Company. The survivors were certain that the pirates were British and closely associated with the British in Bombay. Several recalled the pirates saying that the raid was revenge for what Siddi Yaqut, the Mughal admiral, had done to the British during Child's War, fought between the Company and the Mughals from 1686 to 1690. Also among the passengers on the ship were many women from aristocratic families. It was rumoured that one of them was an elderly woman who was related to Emperor Aurangzeb.

The emperor was furious. He ordered a halt on all foreign trade in territories under the Mughals and imprisoned all the traders in the Surat trading post.

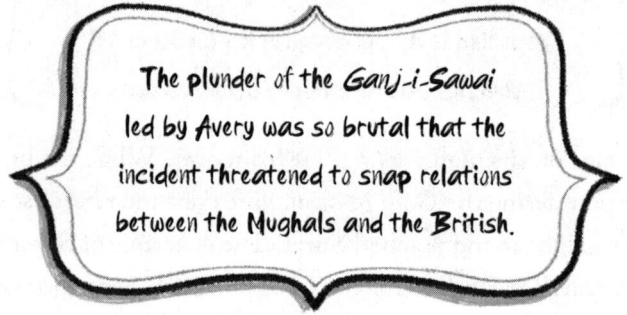

The plunder of the *Ganj-i-Sawai* led by Avery was so brutal that the incident threatened to snap relations between the Mughals and the British.

Aurangzeb was adamant about getting the Europeans to pay for Avery's actions and demanded that all foreign powers trading in India provide an armed escort for Indian ships. The British finally signed an agreement to this effect, bringing an end to a ten-month stand-off.

But this did not end the terror on the seas. News of the raid on the emperor's ship had reached England and the East India Company got the monarch of Britain to place a bounty of

GBP 500 on Avery's head. The Company was under pressure from British traders, who feared for their lives at sea. North America was now a colony of the British and the governor of New York sent out a heavily armed ship called *Adventure*, captained by the Scottish sailor Captain William Kidd, to hunt down the dreaded pirate.

What a twist of fate this turned out to be! Captain Kidd was a privateer, or a private individual who carried out certain actions at sea on behalf of a government. Now privateers were easily tempted by money and riches and, instead of hunting down Avery, Kidd himself became one of the most notorious pirates of all time. He teamed up with a Dutch pirate captain named Dirk Shivers and went on to raid many Indian ships.

Now more furious than ever, Aurangzeb got the Europeans to compensate him for the massive losses to Indian shipping. He also forced them to sign an agreement which made them responsible for all acts of piracy against Indians.

So what happened to Henry Avery?

{ It is said that when the loot from the *Ganj-i-Sawai* was distributed, each of Avery's men received GBP 1,000, in addition to gemstones. }

Back then, this was more money than a sailor could hope to make in an entire lifetime. But the enormous success of their raid had also made them marked men, so the pirates scattered all over the world to avoid being found. Many of them sailed to England's North American colonies, while more than a dozen were hunted down in England and brought to trial in 1696.

But Avery himself had vanished. There are rumours that he lived the rest of his life in poverty in Devon, England. Others claim he fled with a Mughal princess he had stumbled upon on board the *Ganj-i-Sawai*. But this is very unlikely. If he had indeed run away with a woman from the ship, she would have been a Mughal female attendant, not a princess.

It is said the couple had a son called Tom Similaho. He was known to Europeans as Mulatto Tom, since 'mulatto' was a term used to describe a person descended from European pirates and their native wives. Tom went on to found a kingdom in Eastern Madagascar in 1712.

Henry Avery, the greatest thug of Inglistan, remained a free man until his last breath!

VIKRAM SARABHAI AND INDIA'S SPACE ODYSSEY

Today, India's space programme regularly makes headlines around the world. The Indian Space Research Organisation or ISRO is not just sending sophisticated satellites into space; it's making history by sending missions to Mars and beyond. Yes, Indian scientists are crossing the final frontier.

But what makes India's space odyssey so special is its humble beginnings and the inspirational leadership of the man who started it all – Dr Vikram Sarabhai. When Sarabhai founded

India's space programme in the 1960s, competing with countries like the then Union of Soviet Socialist Republics (USSR) and the United States for a top spot in the space race was the last thing on his mind.

> He was dreaming of using satellite technology to take education to rural children and information about the weather to farmers, to help them with their crops. He wanted to harness the power of space technology to transform the lives of ordinary Indians, but it was not easy.

In 1947, India became independent after centuries of colonial British rule, which had drained its wealth. Millions of Indians lived in utter poverty and the country had lost one third of its territory due to the creation of Pakistan. But, still, the country and its leaders dreamt big. Looking at those early days, space scientists at ISRO quote the famous British writer Oscar Wilde: 'We are all in the gutter, but some of us are looking at the stars.'

Dr Vikram Sarabhai, the father of India's space programme, was born into a wealthy industrialist family in Ahmedabad in 1919. His family, the Sarabhais, were among India's biggest textile mill owners. Even though he came from great wealth,

Sarabhai wanted to pursue a career in academics, not business, and earned a PhD from Cambridge, England, in cosmic rays, in 1947.

It was the year of India's independence and Sarabhai persuaded trusts run by family and friends to contribute funds to set up an institute that now conducts research in astronomy, astrophysics, earth sciences and the solar system. Established in 1947, it is called the Physical Research Laboratory. Sarabhai was only in his twenties when he established it.

He had still not hit forty when he began to see a future for India in space. During the International Geophysical Year (IGY) in 1957–58, Sarabhai was India's representative at a convention of international scientists. It was here that the then USSR got the world's attention by announcing the launch of Sputnik 1, the first artificial earth satellite, in October 1957. The space race had begun.

It wasn't long before the United States set up their own space agency called the National Aeronautics and Space Administration (NASA), and China started to develop space technology to create ballistic missiles and weapons.

These developments inspired Sarabhai to launch a space programme for India. But for a country that had only just won its independence and where the majority of the population did not have access to clean drinking water, electricity and toilet facilities, the government wasn't convinced that space research should be a priority.

This did not discourage Sarabhai, who had a very convincing argument for Prime Minister Jawaharlal Nehru. He said the aim of a space programme would not be to explore the moon or put people into space but to use space technology to solve the 'real problems of man and society'.

In other words, India's space programme was founded on humanitarian goals. Sarabhai wanted to use weather and communication satellites to warn people of storms, tsunamis and floods, and to guide rescue and relief services. He also wanted to use satellite television for direct broadcast in villages, to educate children and to get news and information about farming, health, hygiene and family planning, to rural areas.

Nehru was a great believer in modern science and supported Sarabhai's plan. So, in 1962, the government set up the Indian National Committee for Space Research (INCOSPAR). Finally, liftoff! One of INCOSPAR's first tasks was to establish a rocket launch pad station, and since no one in India had any experience with rockets, Sarabhai selected a group of bright young engineers and sent them to NASA for training. They included A.P.J. Abdul Kalam, H.G.S. Murthy and R. Aravamudan, names that will always be associated with the formative years of India's space programme.

> Next, our early space scientists started scouring for a site to set up the launch pad. They discovered that the small fishing village of Thumba, outside Trivandrum in Kerala, had a unique geo-physical phenomenon. It was not only close to the Earth's

magnetic equator, but also to the equatorial electrojet (an electric current system 110 kilometres directly above the equator). This made Thumba perfect for an international rocket launching station.

But there was a problem. When the Department of Atomic Energy acquired one square mile of land in Thumba, there was a church, St Mary Magdalene Church, smack in the middle of it. It was the Bishop of Trivandrum, Rev. Peter Pereira, who persuaded the community to give up the church in the interest of the nation. A new church was built nearby and the original one was used as an office for India's space programme.

The countdown had begun. Since it was early days, India was supported by countries like the United States, the United

Kingdom and West Germany, which provided essential equipment like telemetry receivers, tracking systems and computers. Some of them were loaned and others were gifts.

Finally, time for blast-off! On 21 November 1963, the first sounding rocket (a rocket that takes measurements), supplied by NASA, blasted off from Thumba in the presence of scientists from the United States, the USSR and France – and the bishop who had given up a church to space science.

India had just entered the space age.

After this successful launch, Sarabhai sent a simple telegram home. It read, 'Gee whiz, wonderful rocket show.' Exactly four years later, on 20 November 1967, India launched its first sounding rocket produced in the country. It was called Rohini 75 and its parts were famously transported by bicycle and bullock cart to the launch pad station.

{ Interestingly, Sarabhai was also the pioneer of something we take for granted today – satellite television! }

In 1964, the Tokyo Olympics were transmitted live across the Pacific by an American satellite, Syncom 3. This inspired Sarabhai to set up the Experimental Satellite Communication Earth Station (ESCES) in Ahmedabad. In his paper, *Television for Development* (1969), Sarabhai would write: 'We should consciously reach the most difficult and least developed areas of the country, and because they are in this state, reach them in a hurry.'

And there was no better way to do this than via satellite television. The Indian TV programme, *Krishi Darshan*, launched in 1967, was a part of this initiative. The following year, Sarabhai signed an agreement with NASA to conduct Satellite Television Instructional Experiments (SITE), which were conducted in 1975–76.

> Renowned science writer, Arthur C. Clarke, would later describe SITE as the 'greatest communication experiment in history'.

In 1969, INCOSPAR evolved into India's main space agency, the ISRO, which has since taken Sarabhai's work forward by leaps and bounds. He wanted to use space technology to 'leap-frog our way to development', and he created a foundation to do just that.

Since then, India's space infrastructure has improved the lives of its citizens through telemedicine, remote sensing, geo-mapping, radio networking, mobile communications, meteorological observations and disaster monitoring, all made possible by satellite technology.

Sarabhai died on 30 November 1971, and was given one of India's most prestigious civilian awards, the Padma Vibhushan, after his death, in 1972. A year later, the International Astronomical Union, an association of astronomers, named a crater on the moon after him.

It may have taken a few decades after Sarabhai launched India into space but the country now has an impressive satellite programme, just as he had dreamt. Over time, India's space goals have grown enormously and, in 2014, the country sent up its first Moon Mission and, in 2019, its Mars Orbiter Mission. In 2017, India showed the world that she could become a major player in the multi-billion dollar space market, when ISRO launched a whopping 104 satellites on a single rocket. The earlier record was 37.

So what next? Sending men and women into space? Maybe, for the country is currently training astronauts to explore the great unknown.

It is a matter of great pride that India is constantly pushing the boundaries of the final frontier – all because one man took one giant leap for his country.

THE TASK OF MEASURING INDIA

If you were spending a day at the beach in Madras on 10 April 1802, you would have witnessed a very peculiar sight. An Englishman was supervising an army of porters carrying a giant metal chain, which they were laying out across the beach in a very straight line. The chain was a hundred feet long and its massive links measured around two feet each. It needed twenty porters to carry it.

It gets weirder. The chain was laid in long wooden boxes, in which the porters also placed thermometers. The boxes were balanced on wooden stakes. All the while, the porters had to make sure the chain was stretched perfectly and in a straight line, and this was achieved by a series of props and precision instruments. Finally, a series of tents was erected over the boxes housing the chain.

> What looked like an absurd and clumsy exercise on that April morning more than 200 years ago was the first step in mapping and measuring the Indian subcontinent. It may not have looked like it but this was one of the most scientific exercises of its kind that the world had seen until then. And it was called the Great Trigonometrical Survey of India.

Who would have thought that it would be possible to measure an entire country, that too one as large as India? Besides, in those times, there were no satellites and no computers. You needed porters, clunky instruments and super brains that could perform very complex mathematical calculations. Most of all, you needed plenty of patience and persistence, for the task of measuring India took a good seventy years!

This survey was just one of many different types of surveys undertaken by the British to assess the country. They wanted an accurate idea of the territories and the people they ruled. The information they collected helped them govern better and also make bigger profits from the people and the land.

> The Great Trigonometrical Survey of India began at the end of the Fourth Anglo-Mysore War, with the defeat of Tipu Sultan by the British East India Company in 1799.

Colonel Arthur Wellesley, who led the war for the British, wanted to know exactly how much land they had seized and asked Lt Col. William Lambton (1753–1823), who had served under him in the army, to head the project.

Lambton was an engineer, a mathematician and an astronomer, and had earlier assisted in surveying the boundary between Canada and America. He was more than happy to oblige. The survey was soon extended to the entire Indian subcontinent and the Great Trigonometrical Survey of India began.

Lambton's first task was to calculate the distance from Madras to Mangalore, that is, from the east coast of India to the west coast, because this related to the territories seized from Tipu Sultan. To do this, Lambton needed a baseline or a starting point.

> He established one by using the metal chain to measure the distance between a flagpole on the Madras beach and the grandstand at the Madras Racecourse. By laying out several lengths of the chain one after another, the baseline distance was calculated at 5.85 kilometres, on a flat plain with St Thomas Mount near its northern and Perambalur hill near the southern end.

From the Madras baseline, a series of triangles was calculated using trigonometry and the best instruments of the day, right up to the Mysore plateau. This process was called 'triangulation', the process of determining the location of a point by forming triangles to it from known points.

Lambton and his team of surveyors and porters followed this method by literally walking from hill to hill and pinning the location of each hill they encountered along the way. When Lambton found the plains of the Cauvery delta too difficult to map, he mounted his equipment on temple gateways or gopurams.

> In 1808, when Lambton was surveying the Cauvery delta around Tanjore, he hoisted a giant theodolite, which weighed more than a tonne, on the spire of the famous Brihadeeshwara Temple at Tanjore, at a height of sixty-six metres. As it was about to be placed on the top, the cable snapped and the theodolite came tumbling down. As it fell, it smashed into pieces and knocked off a few pieces of sculpture in the temple. Lambton had to spend a few weeks in Tanjore just to repair his theodolite.

It took him three years but Lambton finally mapped the 660-kilometre, east–west distance from Madras to Mangalore in this way. After all that walking, was he ready to throw in the towel? Not at all. In fact, his ambitions went beyond mapping India. Lambton wanted to calculate the shape or curvature of the Earth itself! This was a topic being hotly discussed and debated by scientists in the Western world at the time, and Lambton felt India could play a central role in answering a fundamental scientific question – was the Earth a perfect sphere or was it, as Isaac Newton had suggested, a little squashed at the poles?

{ Lambton named this project the 'Great Indian Arc of the Meridian'. }

A meridian is any one of the 360 longitudes or invisible lines that run from the north to the south on the Earth's surface. Since the Earth is a sphere, flattened at the poles, each meridian or longitude is curved like an arc. Lambton's Great Indian Arc was a large section of one of the Earth's longitudes.

So from 1811, he set out to map and measure this Great Arc or the 'spine of India', that is, the longitude that connects Kanyakumari, the southernmost point in India, to the Himalayas in the north. It was the longest measurement of the Earth's surface ever to have been attempted.

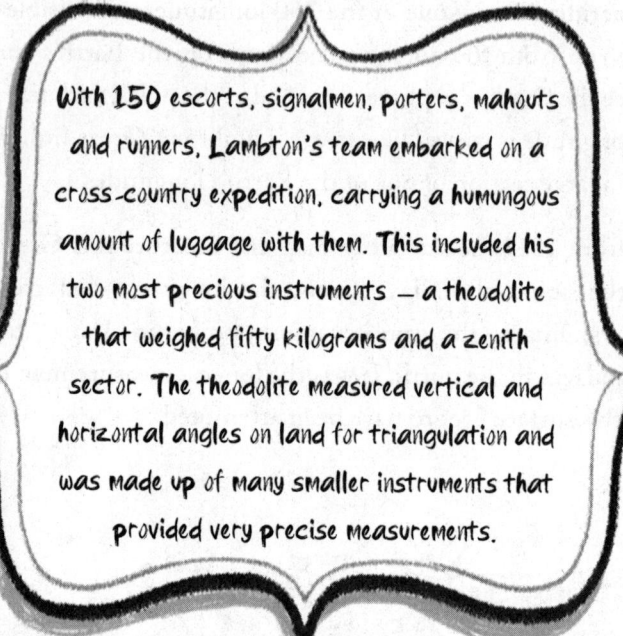

With 150 escorts, signalmen, porters, mahouts and runners, Lambton's team embarked on a cross-country expedition, carrying a humungous amount of luggage with them. This included his two most precious instruments — a theodolite that weighed fifty kilograms and a zenith sector. The theodolite measured vertical and horizontal angles on land for triangulation and was made up of many smaller instruments that provided very precise measurements.

The zenith sector determined the position of the stars relative to land and, in this way, helped calculate the length of a degree of latitude in miles. The zenith sector was basically a telescope attached to a five-foot-long tube that pointed straight up at the skies.

In addition to the massive amount of measuring equipment they had to carry, Lambton's crew also had to haul tents, utensils to cook food and flags to plant atop newly surveyed hills. They had to hack through dense jungles and it sometimes took weeks to travel only a few miles. Wild rivers, wilder animals, deadly insects, heavy rain and infectious diseases also got in the way. Team members often took ill or were injured. Some men even died.

They chased this dream for thirteen years. By 1818, Lambton and his team had travelled from Kanyakumari to Hyderabad, as they walked, measured, recorded and calculated. They had covered an unbelievable 1,020 kilometres, or ten degrees of latitude of the Earth's surface, on foot. What was equally incredible was that Lambton had mapped the south of India with inch-perfect accuracy and an error rate of a mere 0.002 per cent.

He also confirmed that the Earth was not a perfect sphere but had a grapefruit-like shape, a little flattened at the poles. He revised the formula to calculate this shape – one that the great Isaac Newton himself had come up with.

> Lambton was a scientist above all else and all the fame and glory he received for his discovery did not distract him from his goal. He was determined to measure the Great Indian Arc of the Meridian from south to north. So he and his crew set off on the next leg of their survey. With his assistant George Everest and his ever-growing team, Lambton trekked up the length of India towards Nagpur, hoping to eventually reach Agra. He never made it. Lambton died en route, at Hinganghat near Nagpur, in 1823, at the age of seventy.

His work was carried on by George Everest, who completed the Great Indian Arc in 1841, when he arrived at Banog near Mussoorie in the Himalayas. It was 2,400 kilometres long.

But the Great Trigonometrical Survey was far from complete. After Everest, the project to map and measure India was led by two other Englishmen and was eventually completed in 1871. While the British East India Company thought the survey would take about five years, it took nearly seventy years to accomplish. And what a survey it was!

Among its many achievements was the measurement of the height of the Himalayan giants, Mount Everest, K2 and Kanchenjunga. The only other giant who stood just as tall was the man who started it all – Lt Col. William Lambton, who walked the extra mile and astonished the world.

SECTION SEVEN
MORE
QUIRKINESS

THE PLAN TO SELL THE TAJ!

The Taj Mahal in Agra is one of the wonders of the world. So it might seem outrageous, even insane, today, but there was a time when the British actually wanted to sell the monument. Even more shocking, if not a little heartbreaking, is the fact that no one wanted to pay!

This preposterous plan was apparently hatched by the British East India Company in the 1830s, when they needed to raise money after an expensive war had drained the treasury. And the man who concocted this ridiculous scheme was supposedly the governor-general of India Lord William Bentinck (1828–1835) himself. Although Bentinck will be remembered as the statesman who abolished sati or widow sacrifice in India, he also nearly became the most foolish man in history.

The Taj Mahal was built as a mausoleum for Mumtaz Mahal, the beloved wife of Mughal Emperor Shah Jahan, after she died in childbirth in 1631. It is said that the grieving emperor designed the monument himself. The design was so intricate and planned down to the very last detail that it took 20,000 workers, under the supervision of the imperial architects, twenty-two years to complete the complex in 1653. It is said that the Taj Mahal cost a whopping thirty-two million rupees to build. What that would translate to in today's money is hard to imagine!

> Did you know that, distraught by his wife's death, Shah Jahan is said to have cried so much that it damaged his eyes? As a result, he became the first Indian to wear eye glasses, which were chiselled out of a single, flawless diamond known as Halq-e-Noor.

When it was built, the Taj Mahal is said to have had doors of silver, chandeliers of gold studded with jewels and floors covered with priceless Persian carpets. Its grandeur is hard to imagine today! It was such an important building in Mughal times that a special force was created for its protection. This force was under the command of a Faujdar-i-Nawahi or Police Officer of the River Front, and it was set up to protect the Taj Mahal and its waterfront. It even had a naval fleet which patrolled the Yamuna, day and night, to keep the monument safe from thieves and vandals.

{ HALQ-e-NOOR }

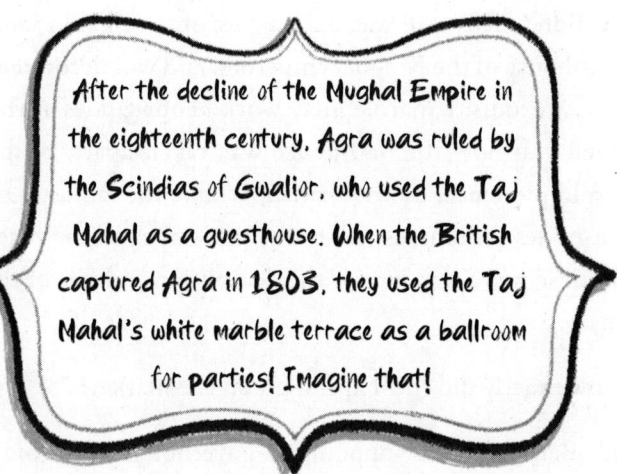

After the decline of the Mughal Empire in the eighteenth century, Agra was ruled by the Scindias of Gwalior, who used the Taj Mahal as a guesthouse. When the British captured Agra in 1803, they used the Taj Mahal's white marble terrace as a ballroom for parties! Imagine that!

Later, it was difficult for even British historians to admit to Bentinck's atrocious plan. They called it a dreadful tale made up by the governor-general's opponents to ruin his reputation. But the plan is clearly mentioned by a handful of British and other European writers in their journals, autobiographies and travel writings. In addition, Indian researchers, like Dr Kavita Singh and even the Archaeological Survey of India (ASI), have written records to prove that such a plan did exist.

Our story begins in Agra, not at the Taj Mahal but two kilometres away, inside the Agra Fort. Step onto the terrace where the Diwan-i-Khas or Hall of Private Audience is located, and you get a sense that something is missing. In a monument whose every detail is carefully crafted, your gaze is drawn to a plain, whitewashed wall with two doors that look very out of place. Why did the craftsmen leave them unfinished?

They didn't. This wall was once a part of the Shahi Hammam or bathhouse of the Mughal emperors, and was decorated with the most exquisite marble inlay work. Tour guides at the fort will tell you how the bathhouse was taken apart, bit by bit, and sold piecemeal by the British. Unlike the fantastic stories these guides sometimes tell, sadly, this one is all too true. The bathhouse was a test run for the demolition and sale of the Taj Mahal!

So how exactly did the Taj end up on the market?

Lord Bentinck was appointed governor-general of India in 1828. The wars in Burma had cost the British East India Company a great deal of money and Bentinck was told to cut costs and improve the finances of the Company. In 1830, when Bentinck set eyes on the Shahi Hammam at the Agra Fort, like everyone else, he too was struck by its beauty. But instead of finding it worthy of preservation, he ordered that the royal bathhouse, along with many colonnades decorated with delicate marble inlay work in the Agra Fort, be dismantled and sold, to raise money for the Company.

> This was not all. Bentinck, it seems, was preparing for something much bigger – the sale of the most magnificent of Mughal monuments, the Taj Mahal itself. Thankfully, the auction of the Agra Fort marble fetched only rock bottom prices. No one really wanted it, and bits and pieces of the royal bathhouse were used to make kitsch and curry stones! Some of the pieces, including Shah Jahan's bathtub,

also made their way to the vaults of the Victoria and Albert Museum in London.

The British community in India was shocked at the goings-on at Agra and one aristocrat and politician, Lord Marcus Beresford, wrote in his *Journal of My Life in India* (1841) that the Agra Fort marble was not suited for use in modern homes. He said a great deal had been purchased but when no one wanted it, it ended up being made into paperweights and other trivial items of daily use for Englishmen. The rich, red sandstone was even used to make curry stones (grinding stones). Lord Beresford added that the demolished bathhouse had fetched no more than 500 pounds.

Another well-known British bureaucrat, Sir William Sleeman, expressed his disbelief at Bentinck's plan. In his autobiography, *Rambles and Recollections of an Indian Official* (1844), he wrote that if the Agra Fort marble had fetched the expected price, 'it is probable that the Taj itself would have been pulled

MADE FROM SHAH JAHAN'S BATHTUB!!

down and sold in the same manner.'

Another person who couldn't believe that the Taj was on the auction block was Fanny Parks. She was a Welsh writer who had travelled extensively in India. In her book, *Wanderings of a Pilgrim in Search of the Picturesque* (1850), Parks included a passage from an article in a British newspaper. Dated 26 July 1831, the article said, 'The Taj has also been offered for sale! But the price required has not been obtained. Two lacs, however, have been offered for it. Should the Taj be pulled down, it is rumoured that disturbances may take place amongst the natives.'

And so, it seems, the plan to sell the Taj Mahal had been set in motion. And guess who its new owner might have been? Parks wrote, 'They say that a Hindoo wishes to buy the Taj to carry away the marble, and erect a temple to his own idols at Bindrabund!'

> This 'Hindoo' was Seth Laxmichand Jain of Mathura, one of the richest bankers in North India. Originally from Malpura in Jaipur, he became a banker to the maharajas and was called 'The Rothschild of India' by the London newspaper, *The Times*.

The story goes that when the British government invited bids for the dismantling of the Taj in 1831, Seth Laxmichand was the highest bidder. He offered Rs 2 lakhs for the monument. But his bid was too low and, at a second auction a few months later, Seth Laxmichand once again emerged as the highest bidder. This time, he offered Rs 7 lakhs. Thankfully, the outrage in the British community and the fear of communal riots breaking out if the Taj Mahal was indeed sold played a part in halting its sale. That's how it was saved.

It wasn't only European accounts that recorded details of this plan. In India, in 2005, the ASI submitted some documents to the Supreme Court of India during its dispute with the Uttar Pradesh Wakf Board, which was making a claim on the Taj. The document produced by the ASI detailed the history of the monument as well as the plan to dismantle and sell it.

Each year, millions of people visit the Taj Mahal and are struck by its sheer beauty. But away from prying eyes, in the vaults of this mausoleum, are the tombs of a queen and her adoring king. This is the world's most enduring monument to love. How can you put a price on that?

PARIS IN PUNJAB

In the heart of Punjab is a petite slice of Paris created by a maharaja obsessed with the City of Light. Well, who isn't just a little in love with Paris? But the maharaja, or should we say 'Monsieur' Jagatjit Singh of Kapurthala, went one step further.

Jagatjit Singh ruled for seventy long years (r. 1877–1947) from his palace in Kapurthala, which is just an hour's drive from Amritsar. But his wasn't just any royal palace. It was built to resemble the Château de Fontainebleau, a medieval castle that was home to many royals in France.

Beyond the palace lay a Greek-style club house, a Moorish-style mosque and a Spanish-style hunting lodge. It was as if the maharaja had recreated the world beyond

{ JAGATJIT SINGH }
MONSIEUR OR MAHARAJA?

in this tiny town in Punjab. To add another touch of glamour, he even built for himself a French chateau with turrets, high up in the hills of Mussoorie.

But even though the maharaja lived it up in his European-style fantasy, he yearned for the real thing. So Jagatjit Singh spent his summers in Paris, where he was quite the star. The French saw him as a very rich and very exotic royal, and they enjoyed his company.

> When he was home, in his palace in Kapurthala, he threw the most lavish parties and entertained European royalty and later American movie stars.

Kapurthala was not always a glamorous princely state on the international social circuit. It was originally a small Sikh principality founded by the Ahluwalia clan, one of many such principalities that emerged in the eighteenth century. The kingdom was established by the fabled Sikh warrior, Baba Jassa Singh Ahluwalia (1718–83).

> He named it after 'Rana Kapu', a prince from Jaisalmer in Rajasthan, who had migrated to Punjab in the tenth century and was an ancestor of the Ahluwalia clan.

By 1809, many of the Sikh principalities had been conquered by Maharaja Ranjit Singh as he carved out the Sikh Empire. But the ruler of Kapurthala and his peers in Patiala and Nabha managed to retain their independence as they turned to the British, who were then ruling India, for protection. Kapurthala was a small kingdom and it became important only after it supported the British during the Revolt of 1857. In return, the British gave the rulers of Kapurthala vast estates, which brought them great wealth and prosperity.

Maharaja Jagatjit Singh ascended the throne in 1877 and his succession was bitterly opposed by a branch of the royal family.

This branch of the family went on to become active supporters of India's freedom movement, and its illustrious members included Rajkumari Amrit Kaur, the first Indian woman cabinet minister in independent India.

But what drew a boy growing up in a feudal and conservative Sikh household in a sleepy kingdom of Punjab, to the wonders of France? It was his childhood love of languages. The maharaja was fluent in English, Persian, Urdu, Gurumukhi and even Sanskrit. But his favourite language was French. And it was through his voracious appetite for French literature and

French books that the young Punjabi prince discovered the world beyond his kingdom. It was a love affair that would last a lifetime.

The maharaja was one of the most well-travelled Indians in the early twentieth century, and that is why people even in the West knew of Kapurthala in India. As he travelled far and wide, visiting places like Morocco, Brazil, Argentina and Japan, Jagatjit Singh wanted to bring the world that he saw abroad back to his people.

In 1905, he commissioned well-known French architect Alexandre Marcel to build him a palace inspired by the French Château de Fontainebleau near Paris. His Kapurthala chateau even had pillars with lapis lazuli! The palace also had a Japanese room, complete with a Samurai warrior suit, a Turkish room and even its very own zoo with a menagerie of exotic animals, such as antelopes, ostriches and zebras. One enclosure contained a pair of Mexican quail, who would eagerly await the maharaja's arrival every morning, excitedly running up and down in their cages when he showed up.

{ Perhaps unparalleled in transport history was Maharaja Jagatjit Singh's 'Zebra Cart', a black-and-white, striped carriage pulled by two zebras. His grandchildren absolutely loved it and they would ride around the palace grounds in this very unusual cart. }

But the maharaja's love for Europe, France in particular, went beyond architecture and the quirky. He wanted to relish the very essence of being French – its cuisine. And, to make sure his chefs could tell their croissants from their coq au vin, Jagatjit Singh sent them to train at the Ritz in Paris. Most incredibly, the royal family drank only specially bottled Evian water, which was shipped from France to Bombay, and then transported by rail from Bombay to Kapurthala!

Once there was fear and paranoia in the palace when the guests' cocktail glasses began to mysteriously empty themselves in the palace drawing room! The mystery was solved when Dr Chang was found sleeping behind the sofas. Dr Chang, the maharaja's prized Pekingese, was the most prominent resident of the palace and a favourite of the maharaja. He was also the snootiest animal imaginable who would turn up his nose at all the overtures to be petted and cuddled. 'Mais tu est méchant! (But you are naughty!),' the maharaja would scold the little dog, while being amazed at his ingenuity.

Apart from his obsession with all things European, Maharaja Jagatjit Singh also wanted to bring the benefits of Europe to his subjects. As a result, Kapurthala was one of the best planned cities in Punjab, with a state-of-the-art water system and other civic facilities. He also built the Jagatjit Club that was inspired by the Acropolis in Athens and the Shalimar Gardens, modelled on the famous Shalimar Gardens in Lahore. A kind and tolerant ruler, he built a gurdwara for his Sikh subjects, a temple for his Hindu subjects and a grand mosque for his Muslim subjects.

> Kapurthala's Moorish mosque is one of the most unique buildings in India. It is a replica of the Grand Mosque in Marrakesh in Morocco, and was designed by a French architect! Its beautiful architecture transports you straight to North Africa.

It was in this spectacular setting that the maharaja entertained visitors from all over the world. It wasn't just très bien; his European guests thought it was fantastique!

But then came Indian independence in 1947 and, with it, the end of an era for Kapurthala. The princely state of Kapurthala merged with the new state of Punjab. Jagatjit Singh died two years later, at the age of seventy-six. The family could no longer afford to maintain such a large palace, and so in 1961, they sold it to the Indian government. It has since been converted into the Kapurthala Sainik School, which trains youngsters aspiring to join the Indian defence forces.

Now only a few outside a select circle remember Kapurthala as it once was – a little piece of Paris in Punjab. How times change. C'est la vie!

HAZARDUARI: PALACE OF ILLUSIONS

Who doesn't love a bit of magic? Now the Nawab of Bengal was no magician but he did have, not one, but 900 tricks up his sleeve. And they still leave visitors to his Hazarduari Palace speechless.

The Hazarduari Palace, or the Palace of a Thousand Doors, is in Murshidabad, the old capital of the nawabs of Bengal, around 180 kilometres north of Kolkata. While, today, it is like any other town in Bengal, with chaotic traffic and a haphazard urban sprawl, in the eighteenth century, Murshidabad was such a beautiful city that it rivalled mighty capitals such as Paris, London and Vienna. European travellers who visited it were so impressed by its size and beauty that they considered it one of the greatest cities they had ever seen.

> It was a small worm — the silkworm — that made Murshidabad one of the richest cities in the world of its time. The abundance of silkworms in the area and the high quality of silk they produced drew traders from all around the world to the city, from the Armenians and Greeks to the English and French.

Murshidabad became the capital of the nawabs when, after the decline of the Mughal Empire in the eighteenth century, the Mughal governor of Bengal, Murshid Quli Khan, shifted his capital here from Dhaka. With the nawabs came the nobles, bankers, artists, poets and painters, and soon palaces, mosques, temples, gardens and mansions filled the city.

The great riches of Bengal made the Murshidabad Mint the most important mint in India, and it controlled the riches of the East. In the centre of the city was a great fort, known as Qila Nizamat, which was the main seat of the nawabs.

But its wealth and power also made Murshidabad a hotbed of jealousy and intrigue. In 1756, Siraj-ud-Daulah succeeded his grandfather, Alivardi Khan, as the Nawab of Bengal. He was only twenty-three years old and the brash young Siraj was not always liked by his powerful relatives and nobles. He also fell out with the British East India Company, when he attacked Fort William in Calcutta and demolished its walls.

> This incident sparked many conspiracies against the nawab and it finally led to the historic Battle of Plassey in 1756, which ended in defeat for Siraj-ud-Daulah.

The nawab had been betrayed by his commander Mir Jafar, who had been bribed by the British. The East India Company, under Robert Clive, seized control of Murshidabad, got rid of Siraj-ud-Daulah and made Mir Jafar the Nawab of Bengal.

With the British in control and Mir Jafar their puppet, Murshidabad lost its importance. Traders and merchants migrated to Calcutta, which became the capital of British East India Company's Indian territories. What remained in Murshidabad was the nawab's court, which enjoyed no real power.

But the nawabs were allowed to keep their palaces, the royal court and material possessions so that they could feel important. But behind the scenes, there was usually someone plotting to overthrow the nawab, either the British, his rivals or even someone within the royal court.

> The greatest symbol of Murshidabad's powerless court was the Hazarduari Palace, which was built by Nawab Nazim Humanyun Jah, who ruled from 1824 to 1838. It is called 'Hazarduari' because it has 1,000 doors ('hazar' meaning 'a thousand' and 'duari' referring to 'doors'). But get this – only 110 doors are real. The rest are an amazing illusion!

While no one knows for sure why the palace has so many fake doors, historians believe it was to confuse and trap intruders, spies and others who might have wanted to harm the nawab, who had probably dreamt up an elaborate security feature for his Hazarduari Palace. Bengal was one of the richest regions in India and, despite his loss of power, the nawab was so wealthy, he could build almost anything he wanted, including a palace with almost a thousand fake doors!

FAKE OR REAL?

The Hazarduari Palace stands in an area known as Qila Nizamat, the old fort, which has now all but disappeared. It was designed by a British architect named Duncan McLeod in European style. The palace took eight years to build, from 1829 to 1837, is three stories high and the size of an entire city block. It has 114 rooms. Its grand stone staircase is probably the largest in India (the lowermost step is 108 feet wide) and the crystal chandelier in the Durbar Hall is colossal.

In front of the palace is a great cannon with a very peculiar name – Bacchawali Tope, or the cannon which gives birth to a child. This cannon once protected the city from invaders. The legend goes that it was fired only once and made such a din that pregnant women in the city gave birth in fright. This is how the cannon got its name.

In front of the palace is a clock tower nicknamed the Big Ben of Murshidabad.

{ It was designed by Sagore Mistri, the assistant to McLeod, the architect of the palace. }

Near the palace were also the nawab's stables, called the astabal, where hundreds of the nawab's finest horses were kept. A giant, steam-powered engine would prepare the feed for the

Bacchawali Tope

horses, and a great clock would tell the time so that the horses could be fed on time. Sadly, all these have disappeared.

The Hazarduari Palace turned out to be a lavish waste. It was only used for durbars (official meetings), ceremonies and as a guest house for visiting British officials. The later nawabs were even critical of it. Apparently, they felt its Italianate architecture did not suit an Indian prince. Besides, the palace was considered too small. The royal family had always lived in the numerous mansions they owned around the palace. Turns out, the fake doors served no purpose!

Today, the Hazarduari Palace is a museum run by the Archaeological Survey of India and it has some spectacular antiques on display. But its most intriguing exhibits, we think, are the ones in its walls.

ABOUT THE AUTHORS

Live History India, which is part of Peepul Tree World, is India's fastest growing digital platform dedicated to the subcontinent's rich history. With a network of over 150 historians and archaeologists across the country, www.livehistoryindia.com goes deep within India, digging into its history to bring alive the many fascinating 'Stories that Make India'. The stories in this book have been written by LHI's team of researchers. The team includes **Akshay Chavan, Aditi Shah, Carol Lobo, Deepanjan Ghosh** and **Kurush Dalal**. This book has been edited and curated by Live History India's Editor **Mini Menon**.

Mini Menon   Akshay Chavan

Aditi Shah   Carol Lobo

Deepanjan Ghosh   Kurush Dalal

ABOUT THE ILLUSTRATOR

Tanvi Bhat is a self-taught children's book illustrator who, on sunny days, also moonlights as an author. She has a huge line-up of work creating pictures for some of India's top publishers. Tanvi loves working with a variety of mediums such as watercolours, colour pencils and gouache. Always working with her hands, she is constantly scribbling ideas on scraps of paper that she promptly loses. Tanvi is a foodie and a zine creator, too.

ALSO FROM LIVE HISTORY INDIA

Selected for the Parag Honour List 2021

Eccentric maharajas and nawabs, bizarre believe it or not tales and hilarious twists and turns come together in this first book of the Quirky History series …

From the Nizam who hid a priceless diamond in a shoe, to the Maharaja of Nabha with his bizarre Swan Car, to the Nawab of Junagadh whose dog Roshanara was married in brocades and pearls with over 700 guests in attendance, and many more quirky, unusual stories.

Get ready for history to pop right out of this book!

THE QUIRKY HISTORY SERIES

The Quirky History series is an effort to offer readers a taste of our amazing history and help them enjoy, appreciate and love the many known and unknown stories that make India what it is — a land of beauty, wealth and so many hidden wonders! This mission is at the very heart of Live History India.

The first book in the series is *The Swan Car of Nabha & Other Unusual Stories from History*.

The second book in the series is *Strange Stories from History*.

30 Years *of*
HarperCollins*Publishers*India

At HarperCollins, we believe in telling the best stories and finding the widest possible readership for our books in every format possible. We started publishing 30 years ago; a great deal has changed since then, but what has remained constant is the passion with which our authors write their books, the love with which readers receive them, and the sheer joy and excitement that we as publishers feel in being a part of the publishing process.

Over the years, we've had the pleasure of publishing some of the finest writing from the subcontinent and around the world, and some of the biggest bestsellers in India's publishing history. Our books and authors have won a phenomenal range of awards, and we ourselves have been named Publisher of the Year the greatest number of times. But nothing has meant more to us than the fact that millions of people have read the books we published, and somewhere, a book of ours might have made a difference.

As we step into our fourth decade, we go back to that one word – a word which has been a driving force for us all these years.

Read.

Harper Collins

4th

HARPER PERENNIAL

HARPER BUSINESS

HARPER BLACK

हार्पर हिन्दी

HarperCollins *Children's Books*

HARPER DESIGN

HARPER VANTAGE

Harper Sport